# A CHAIRMAN'S YEAR

## In the Service of my County

### A PERSONAL ACCOUNT OF ONE YEAR IN THE OFFICE OF CHAIRMAN OF LEICESTERSHIRE COUNTY COUNCIL

*by Ernie White*

A CHAIRMAN'S YEAR
IN THE SERVICE OF MY COUNTY



Published in 2017
by Ernie White
4 Middleton Close
Stoney Stanton
Leicester LE9 4TS

ISBN 978-0-9929085-2-2

# Contents

# Chapter One
# A Lad from Leicester

I was born and brought up in Leicester. I was born with a happy heart. Leicester is my home and the source of all my interests, I went to junior and grammar school in the city, I studied, late in life, for degree qualifications at the, then, Leicester Polytechnic, now De Montfort University. Though born in Braunstone, I was brought up in the south of the City just off the Saffron Lane, near 'the banks', which gave walking access to the three premier sporting venues, Filbert Street for football, Welford Road for rugby and Grace Road for cricket, and lots of other attractions for a small boy growing up in the aftermath of the war years. So, as a very young boy, I watched football at Filbert Street, though never paying to get in because we used to dodge under the turnstiles, during the late forties and early fifties, when the City were an up and down team.

I remember 1949 and being lifted up to my Mothers shoulders when the team came home after the cup final defeat at the hands of Wolves. I remember Gordon Banks making his debut and then, later, the very young Peter Shilton followed in his footsteps. I remember some characters who stay in the memory long after the names of their often more gifted team mates have been forgotten. Derek Dougan for instance, Willie Gardiner, a Scotsman with a temper but he certainly knew where the goal was, and one of the most gifted players ever, in my opinion, to play for city, David Gibson. The best times for the City in my memory, before the Martin O'Neil years,

Grammar School 1953

was the Jimmy Bloomfield era, a good footballing team with real characters playing in it, playing very attractive football.

I watched the 'Tigers' play at the Welford Road ground when the boundary with Aylestone Road was a huge red brick wall with tall trees with thick trunks along the outside and any agile boy would merely shin up between the trees and the wall and hop over the top to watch good rugby. The County Cricket ground was also near so it was familiar territory to me anyway but I came to know it well because it was also my grammar school playing field. Whilst at City Boys School, on those occasions when the County were playing at home our games periods were cancelled and we were made to sit and watch the game and sometimes we worked the scoreboards.

I remember watching Charlie Palmer bat and cannot forget getting changed in the wooden stand with the old showers in the basement and the very worn wooden seats so that you often got splinters in your feet.

I knew how to get in to watch cricket by sliding sideways two planks of wood from the fencing along the 'black pad', a footpath that runs alongside the ground.

I had aunts and uncles all over the City, in Belgrave, in Braunstone on Eyres Monsell, though that was still fields when I was a small boy, Coleman Road, along Saffron Lane, along Thurcaston Road, in New Parks as well as a branch of the family spread all across Loughborough. My Aunties used to push me around Abbey Park when I was a baby in a pushchair and we spent many Sundays happily walking in Bradgate Park.

Memorable Christmas's, when the whole family gathered at Grandma's house on Wyville Row, and we children had to share the one or two beds.

Where we lived, at the bottom end of Saffron Lane, was in many ways ideal because as well as being close to all the sporting venues we were also within walking distance of the bright lights of the City. Yet the countryside was also just around the corner whether, at the top of Saffron Lane or just along the Aylestone Road. The canal at Aylestone was handy for fishing and general messing about, I remember sitting at the weir near the mill race at Aylestone and watching Ivan Marks, practice the craft that eventually saw him fish for England on many occasions.

A walk along the towpath meant a visit to Aylestone boathouse, or right through bluebell woods to Blaby Wharf. Sometimes we would walk from home to where grandma lived on Wyville Row in Braunstone, stopped at the tea rooms along what was then Coalpit Lane, it's called Middleton Street now, for a glass of lemonade and on the way back at the boathouse for an ice cream and another drink. Sometimes, when I was very small, I remember we did not walk back along the towpath but carried on to the top of Coalpit Lane, where it joined the Aylestone Road at what was called Aylestone Junction where we would catch a tram, with slatted wooden seats that were very smooth which made it difficult to avoid slipping along them when the tram stopped, to the Hughendon Drive stop just before the gas works.

I remember when the war ended being taken along Saffron Lane by my mother to see the street lights on, the first time I would have seen the 'lane' lit up, and I was five years old!

We were handy for the gas works too, and this was a real bonus in 1947 when we lads, and I was only six years old, would collect a convoy of old prams and trolleys and queue for hours from early morning on a Saturday to collect coke during that long hard winter and take it round to the old people or anybody else who found it impossible to collect it for themselves.

Across the road from our house was the allotment gardens on Saffron Lane and across Saffron Lane was the wartime army camp, a vast and open site, it became the Saffron Lane Sports Centre, and just along the Aylestone Road was the Freemens Common, then a huge expanse of allotment gardens laid out in a grid system with roads identified as Road A, Road B and so on. The whole area was bordered by Saffron Lane, Aylestone Road, the cattle market and Welford Road and the main line railway.

The Cattle Market itself kept us occupied all day on market day, there was always something going on, the slaughterhouses, the auction ring which was built like a small arena with raised tiers of seats around a small ring, the small animal market, chickens, rabbits, turkeys and almost any other small creature that could be traded.

At the back of the cattle market was access to either Freemans Common or Knighton Junction and the Knighton tunnel and this area had everything a gang of small boys could wish for, offering endless opportunities for mischief in general and scrumping and birds nesting in particular. If you knew the way there was also a small newt pond hidden from the main view and this was wonderful because no one knew where you were which added to the mystery and the fun. Just outside the old cattle market gates, where a garage showroom is now was an old water pump with a long handle, just right on hot summer days when we had been roaming all over Freemans Common and were feeling hot and tired.

We scrumped apples and other fruit mainly and generally played the game of watching for 'the bloke' to leave his allotment before taking some fruit and sometimes other things like fresh potatoes to roast. Even now I can remember the taste of scrumped potatoes roasted black as cinders in a fire and eaten with scrumped 'goosegogs' or gooseberrys and blackberries. Delicious!

Opposite our house was the brook and around the corner and along Saffron Lane were the two parks, the 'big' and the 'little' park, just up Knighton Fields Road was the Aylestone swimming baths where I learnt to swim and where we could spend all day in the water on a Saturday and watch as the footballers and rugger players from the pitches on the park joined us at the end of their match.

I remember watching the first diesel locomotive No. 00001 pass across the bridge over Knighton Fields Road, excited by the newness of it and not realising that they signalled the end of the steam trains and the magic of train spotting.

We, our little 'gang' that is, all had the books of numbers and names for each region, LMS, or London Midland Scottish, LNER or London North Eastern Railway, GWR the Great Western Railway and the others, and marked the books when we spotted numbers and names. Hundreds and hundreds of locomotives with exotic names like the Gilbert and Ellice Islands or The Seychelles, lists of regiments of the British Army like The Green Howards, The Irish Guards, The Highland Fusiliers among many others.

Some of these we 'plated' on London Road Station when, providing the driver was not looking, we would jump onto the footplate, a great coup, which meant we could mark the entry for that locomotive with a 'P'.

A childhood spent in Leicester makes the City mine I am part of it and part of me is in it, it is my home and my alma mater

I have set my Leicester roots down in some detail because I have often heard it said that because people like me serve on the

County Council we shouldn't be commenting on City matters. I have just as much right as anyone else to comment about my home town, the place I was born and brought up and the place I know well, the good and the bad.

Leicester is not a pretty city in the way that parts of Nottingham and Birmingham are, it is not a great city the way that Manchester or Leeds can claim to be, but it is a City of working people, an honest City, a City of good people and a City I am happy to call my own.

I left the City when I got married in the early sixties because you could then only buy an affordable house in the suburbs. Then when any young couple got engaged they usually made a beeline for Jelsons Office or a site office and put down a deposit on one of the hundreds of Jelson houses springing up in every area of the County.

I left the City, not by free choice but by force of circumstance, and initially we bought a house in Blaby and after a few years there we moved to Stoney Stanton when I found a job in Earl Shilton. I took to Stanton immediately and have never regretted the move and despite several changes in employment since have never brought myself to consider moving away. So when the opportunity was offered, surprisingly, for me to represent the area on the County Council in 1975, despite having no background in council affairs I was proud and privileged to put my name forward, and felt very privileged to be elected.

Long before I became involved in local politics or indeed a member of the County Council I recall many times wondering about the various mayors and other dignitaries who opened things and attended official functions and made speeches. Along with many members of the general public my knowledge of civic affairs and what a Mayor or Chairman does was sadly lacking. Most of what goes on in the Council Chamber, be it the local parish, town or district council or the larger and more important County Council is largely ignored by the vast majority of the electorate.

I have always felt saddened by this because once elected a councillor operates only on behalf of those he represents yet those he represents seem not to care what he or she actually does. So when the opportunity was offered to me after 20 years or so service as a Councillor to serve the County of Leicestershire, initially for a year as Vice Chairman and then a year as

Chairman I thought very carefully about what it was that I wanted to do with the office and further more, that I would let the electorate know what I intended to do and then let them know what I had done, a sort of one man PR effort for the County Council and the many and varied services that it provided for the public of Leicestershire.

I had always been impressed by the vast store of knowledge and expertise that the local civil service, the officers of the County Council, at all levels could offer across the whole array of disciplines. I always knew that whatever I needed to know about any aspect of Government legislation across all the services that somewhere within the County Council would be someone who could tell me and tell me willingly and with enthusiasm.

There were thousands of employees whose priority was simply to serve the citizens of Leicester and Leicestershire, in schools, in old folk's homes, in trading standards, in highways and transportation, in museums and libraries. Even after all the changes that had impacted on the way councils delivered services I found that the overriding ethos across all departments was to deliver services to people where and when they were needed.

This is not always appreciated by a general public seemingly oblivious of the commitment to this goal and who are only too often eager and well prepared to criticise, and grumble about the cost or the level of services. All too often public opinion polls reveal a strong desire on the part of the public to pay lower local taxes yet still demand better and better services. It was the job of the employees of the County Council to attempt to square this circle and always in the glare of publicity.

I wanted to highlight the breadth and depth of what the County Council did for the general public of Leicestershire day in day out, week in week out, often to a very high standard and all too often with the willing commitment of our employees who generally did much more than they were paid for because of the strength of devotion to the cause of public service.

So, I set out to mark my Chairman's year as a year when I would do what I could to show the human face of the County Council to everyone in the County and to try to celebrate the ethos of public service and bring to the notice of the County residents all the various services that they receive from the County Council.

# CHAPTER TWO
# LEICESTERSHIRE COUNTY COUNCIL.

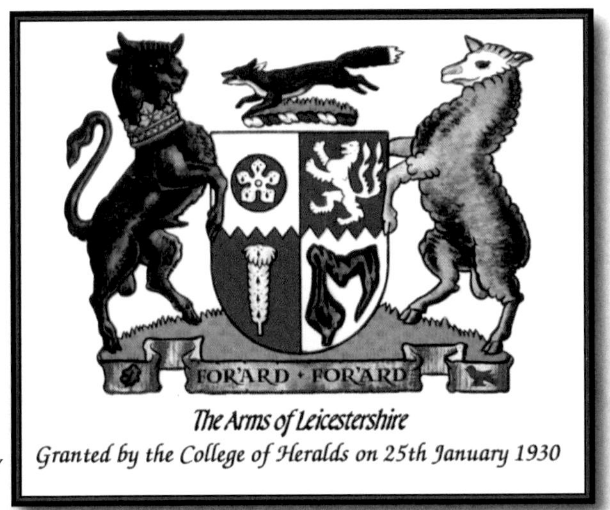


*The Arms of Leicestershire*
*Granted by the College of Heralds on 25th January 1930*

THE COUNTY CREST

In 1994, the year I began my 'civic' life as Vice Chairman of the Council, the County Council was a very large organisation, though smaller now due to the 1997 changes, which took out of it the City of Leicester and the County of Rutland. In fact it was then, as now, really a collection of different departments, many of which have almost nothing in common with the others. I had set myself the task of bringing to the attention of the public the work of all the departments of the County Council during my year as Chairman. The work of some of the departments is very high profile and attracts public attention for both positive and negative reasons. Education for instance being a subject on which there is significant political controversy is almost never out of the news.

Social Services, as it was then called, also gets a lot of media attention, as do the issues surrounding highways and road building. However there are also other very important services that were delivered by the County Council some almost unnoticed by the general public, but nonetheless managed in a thoroughly professional and cost effective way.

In any Chairman's year there would be natural opportunities for bringing to the attention of the public the work of many departments, openings, speech days, festivals and other special events. Having made the theme of my year the work of the departments there were many engagements arranged specially for me to show support for departmental initiatives.

I was determined also to visit all the departments and try to get the media to give some attention to the work of the lesser known ones so as to give public recognition to the staff for the important work that they did.

## The Education Service

Since I was first elected to the Council in 1975 I had always been involved in the Education Committees at County Hall and had seen many changes. Andrew Fairbairn had been Director of Education for most of my time and is probably the best known of the Directors to have served the post 1973 County Council. He was fiercely loyal to his service and strongly committed to the Leicestershire Plan and Community Education and was much respected by all his staff in return. He was also a consummate politician and renowned for being well in control of the committees of the education service. He was without doubt the last of the autocratic heads of service and exercised enormous influence and control over every aspect of the County's education system. How the role and influence exercised by the Director has declined since I was first elected is a measure of how far national government has now taken control of the education service.

If you consider that in 1975 in Leicestershire the Education Department administered one Polytechnic, one teacher training college at Scraptoft, one agricultural training college, an Arts College, six colleges of further education, an Adult Education College, all the Community Colleges, all the Upper Schools, all the High Schools and all the Primary Schools. It employed all the teachers, selected all the heads and employed a huge number of curriculum advisers. It ran an inspection unit, maintained all the buildings. It ran the youth service, the careers service and the special education service and provided all the school meals.

It owned and managed an outdoor pursuits centre in Wales, owned Beaumanor Hall and some other primary centres, maintained the twinning links in France, Italy and Germany as well as supported the School of Music, the School of Dance and Drama, and of course the structure that supported the county system of Comprehensive Community Education. It also managed the student grant service, a major undertaking in those days. It had its own finance and personnel unit so that it was a mini empire within the County Council itself.

ABERGLASLYN HALL

Andrew Fairbairn was renowned for his attention to the development of talented heads and prospective heads and attended most of the interviews for headship appointments, and for those he could not attend personally he made sure that one of his senior colleagues went instead and reported back to him.

The Directors that followed him were bedevilled by constant changes imposed by successive governments. Keith Wood-Allum, the immediate successor to Andrew Fairbairn caught the first wave of far reaching government changes and saw the work of the department severely reduced firstly by a series of actions which took the Polytechnic, the Colleges of Further Education, the Sixth Form Colleges, advice and inspection, careers advice, some schools that took the Grant Maintained route, out of control of the County Council, most of which were handed over to quangos.

Central Government then forced local education authorities to delegate the spending of 85% of the total education budget to individual schools under the Local Management of Schools legislation, and then under what came to be known as the purchaser/provider split, the department was divided up into business units and each of them had to 'sell' their services to schools. This process caused the loss of something like 400 jobs in the department and was responsible for a significant loss of morale among the remaining members of staff.

During my year of office the Director of Education was Jackie Strong, who took over at a very difficult time for the department and would also have to steer the department through the traumas of Local Government Reform which would see all the City schools become the responsibility of the new Leicester City Council in 1997.

I had made a point of making a number of visits to a variety of schools across the County whilst I was Vice-Chairman, including the special schools. Some schools and heads were not sure what such visits were for, some were slightly suspicious as though I were some kind of one person inspection unit but the vast majority saw the visits for what they were, an attempt by a member of the authority in civic, not political office, showing an interest in how schools were coping during a period of great change and uncertainty.

## Planning and Transportation

One of the largest departments is the Department of Planning and Transportation which covered a whole range of services from highway maintenance, highway design, road building, structure planning, economic development, traffic monitoring, training, street lighting, waste management, minerals planning and development.

With Tommy and Mrs
Thompson. 1995–96

I remember the early days of my membership of the council when Mr Sherriffs was Director. He was succeeded by Donald Sabey who gave way to Tommy Thompson who was director during my year as Chairman. He was also for that year the President of the County Surveyors Society, a great honour for both 'Tommy' and the County Council.

## The Department of Property

One of the smaller but highly efficient departments within County Council was undoubtedly the Department of Property. The department was responsible for the maintenance and upkeep of the building stock, the design and construction of new buildings, leasing, valuation and the buying and selling of County owned property. The department had been under performing for some time and it was only when Peter Smith, who was the Director of Property whilst I was Chairman, became chief officer that the department developed into one of the best run departments of the County Council.

For some strange reason the department also had responsibility for the running of Bosworth Park and the Ancient Battlefield site and the visitor centre as well as Watermead Park, that vast area of the Soar Valley that was in the ownership of the County Council.

Very early in my term of office I had laid plans to visit all the departments and it was during this visit that I became aware of the professional and dedicated team of officers that Peter Smith had around him. State of the art processes for controlling energy in our buildings, all the latest computer technology applied to building design and maintenance schedules, all delivered by a very efficient department using modern management techniques on a very modest budget. Peter was the model of a modern local government officer, immersed in the ethos of public service yet committed to effective and efficient user of resources.

The main contact with the department was for the commemoration of the Battle of Bosworth at Bosworth Park and the enormous assistance they gave me for the fishing contest that I organised to raise funds for the Sir Andrew Martin Trust for Young People.

## Social Services Department

I had never served on the other of the 'main three' service committees, the Social Services Committee, mainly because at the time I was first elected my mother was a serving Home Help, and I would have been declaring an interest in many debates, so I never put myself forward to serve on the committee, even after Mother retired I always avoided being nominated. I remember that the Director then was Dorothy Edwards, who I thought was a rather intimidating woman with whom I had very little contact.

I recall one occasion when I was a very new councillor and very green, being summoned to her office in the presence of Neville Hanger, who was then Chairman of the Committee, as well as the Conservative group whip, to be 'scolded' for asking questions about a case involving a mother with new born twins and one other child under one year old, who had sought some help from Social Services when she felt unable to manage the workload her young children imposed on her. One of the twins had been taken into care, which I thought a bit extreme. Mrs Edwards clearly thought I was getting above myself by questioning the decisions of the professionals.

When Dorothy Edwards retired she was succeeded by Brian Rice who was to gain some notoriety during the dreadful affair of the child abuse scandal in the late 1980s. The strangest aspect of that affair was that only a handful of senior elected members had a clue as to how serious this was. I recall being told by a journalist that it was likely to be the biggest child abuse case in history, though I could hardly believe him as the matter had not been discussed by councillors at all.

After Brian Rice left, Leicestershire was fortunate to find the perfect man to lead the Department through the morale-sapping aftermath of the Beck affair and after two or three years the department regained its self-confidence. Brian Waller was the man responsible and he served the County Council well until he too took early retirement along with a number of gifted Chief Officers on Local Government Reorganisation in 1997. Some of the most enjoyable engagements I undertook as Chairman were to perform the reopening ceremony for a number of elderly person's homes after they had been refurbished, as well as attending some 100th birthday celebrations.

I also tried to visit some of the more obscure facilities that Social Services were responsible for, from abandoned women to young offenders, and as always the interest of the Chairman seemed to be appreciated by staff, many of whom worked with very difficult young people on a day to day basis and often wondered whether anyone knew they were there.

## Eastern Shires Purchasing Organisation

A little known success story was The Eastern Shires Purchasing Organisation or ESPO as it is always known as within County Hall, which is a consortium of East Midland local authorities whose combined purchasing power has brought great savings for the local taxpayer over the years. Highly professional and well led since its formation this is one department that operated very successfully in a private sector environment.

## Library Department

Geoffrey Smith was the Director of Libraries for many years and developed the service though the aftermath of the 1973 changes. John Hinks, his successor was not quite as high profile as Geoffrey Smith had been, but an effective Director nevertheless.

## Museums Department

Patrick Boylan was the Director of Museums when the new County Authority was formed in 1973 and thanks to some creative thinking a rather unique service was formed. The new City Council declined to register as a Museums Authority, which left the County Council free to run a countywide service. I had no idea when I was elected, nor for some time afterwards, what a fine service this had become. Patrick Boylan laid the foundations and it was not until I came to know his successor Tim Schadla-Hall that I came to understand that all the Museums across the City and County were part of one service, so that the collective quality of the service was far greater than the sum of all the buildings and the collections, and able to employ a full range of professional specialists to run a comprehensive service.

It worked, and worked well, on behalf of the people of Leicester and Leicestershire and Rutland come to that. I came to realise too that it worked very well under the leadership of Tim Schadla Hall. My first contact with 'Tim' came about through an article I had written in the County Councils Gazette in which I was critical of the Thatcherite attitude to Local Government. Tim wrote me a rather nice note after he had read it, and after I telephoned him to say thank you we came to understand that we had things in common, mainly about local government.

I had not served on the Museums Committee, or to give it its full name Arts, Libraries and Museums Committee, and so I was not involved in the initial planning for the creation of Snibston Discovery Park, an innovative and exciting new 'museum' to be built on the derelict Snibston Colliery site in Coalville. It was a project initiated by Patrick Boylan but Tim Schadla-Hall was the chief officer who made it happen, though much of the day-to-day planning was done by his deputy, Heather Broughton, and I only became involved when there was talk within the Conservative group of scrapping the project to save money.

I thought the move to stop it, or privatise it, was wrong and I was not convinced by the arguments being put forward for not proceeding with the project. So I rang Tim Schadla-Hall and asked if someone could brief me about the project and the issues involved. Without hesitation he himself agreed to meet me on site to give me the details and to answer any questions. So one July afternoon we both 'yomped' across the tip mounds of this derelict and abandoned mine site, though the main building had been started and was beginning to take shape.

As Tim explained the plans and the ideas for this new museum, and there have not been too many of those from the public sector lately so it was probably unique, I realised that he knew what he was doing and would make it work.

The Museum department was full of talented people, it was also very well managed and the staff felt a great sense of loyalty to the department and to Tim Schadla-Hall too. He also developed a service driven by the needs of its customers, that also involved staff at all levels as well as elected members, who quickly 'went native', and as I was one of them I know that this caused some other members to be very suspicious because they thought that we put the interests of the department above that of the taxpayer. It wasn't really like that of course, it just meant that we knew more about the museum service than most others members knew about any other part of the councils services. It was a positive not a negative thing.

Tim and I and many others worked very hard together to stop the Museums Service becoming a casualty of the Local Government Review, but in the event we failed to save the service and Tim was to join the many other gifted chief officers who were forced to take early retirement in 1997 and so were paid well by way of compensation ***not*** to serve the public of Leicestershire, and who are now lost to local government as well.

## The Police Service (as it was in 1995/6)

The police service was removed from the oversight of the County Council during my term of office, a move I thought unnecessary. So, instead of the Police Service being a central part of a local democratically elected authority it was floated off to become a free standing quango with members of the police authority now appointed by the Home Secretary instead of being elected local politicians nominated by colleagues. Previously the Chairman of the Police Committee would therefore be a serving County Councillor so everyone knew who he or she was, and who could be questioned either at Committee or at any meeting of the full County Council.

Additionally an aggrieved member of the public had a figure-head to complain to, the press had access to someone who was accountable to the local electorate and it worked. Nowadays I guess that very few people know who the Chairman of the Police Authority is, and the new police authority spends enormous amounts of time and money holding area meetings as pretence at accountability. Neither system is perfect, both have weaknesses, but because under the former system the Chief Constable, every two months, had to report to a committee of locally elected and accountable local politicians the police service was cemented into the locality it served, it was a healthier and more open system.

The Chairman of the County Council comes into contact with the Chief Constable very frequently, and in the year in which I was Chairman this was an added pleasure because the Chief Constable was very good company. Keith Povey was very down to earth, had a very good sense of humour and we shared many good moments.

## Fire and Rescue

The Fire and Rescue Service is yet another of the services that had been under the umbrella of the County Council since 1973 but earmarked for change in the same way as the Police Authority.

I had not known Bob Rawlinson, who was Chief Fire Officer when I was elected in 1975, and did not get to know his successor Norman Dickerson well until I became Chairman. He ran a service that was highly regarded, not just locally but nationally, in which there was a tremendous spirit of camaraderie, as might be expected in a group of men and women who sometimes risked their lives and relied on each other in dangerous situations.

We enjoyed the company of Norman Dickerson, and Mrs Dickerson (Avril) at a number of events over the course of the two years that we were involved in civic affairs.

## Trading Standards

Trading Standards is another 'Cinderella' department of the County Council and one that just gets on with serving the public in a highly professional way day in, day out, week in, week out, and yet the public hardly notice. I guess if a poll was conducted about the service the vast majority of people would have no idea that it was a County Council service. Richard Peck was Chief Officer and like so many other chief officers ran a good department driven by the ethos of serving the public.

The department is responsible for the regulatory services necessary to ensure that the Sale of Goods Acts, Weights and Measures Acts, Consumer Protection Laws, Road Traffic Acts and a host of other Acts of Parliament that protect the public were enforced

## County Secretary's Department

The County Secretary's Department is a key department within the County Council, it is both the legal department and also the department that clerks all the committee's. Tim Harrison was County Secretary over most of the time I have been an elected member, though until I became Chairman I did not have much to do with the department. Tim Harrison always sat next to the Chairman during meetings of the County Council and so was always on hand to give advice about procedure and standing orders. He was always supposed to time the speeches so that the Chairman could be told when a member had used his alloted time. I say supposed because on more than one occasion the timer seemed not to be working so sometimes a member was given more time than standing orders allowed.

## The Office of the Chief Executive

Most important is the Chief Executive's Department and although each of the departments has a Chief Officer or Director and a management structure, including personnel, accounting and finance of its own, they all operate within the corporate structure of the council and the responsibility for overseeing this corporate structure falls to the Chief Executive. Just after I was elected Sam Jones was appointed as Chief Executive and during the time he was in post he left his signature all over the County Council.

After the 1981 County Council election Leicestershire was the first County Council to have no party in overall control and it is down to Sam Jones, and the rest of the senior officer team, that this fundamental change in control was managed so well. This situation didn't end until 2001.

The Council conducted its business then without any cross party alliances or pacts or deals, so the job of the officers is all that more difficult. The one thing that officers need is for members to deliver policies and decisions as quickly as possible. In Leicestershire this rarely happened so the Chief Executive had to hold the ring, ensure parity in the supply of information to members and not become embroiled in the day-to-day political bickering. Sam did this with some style. He also saw the need for the County Council to develop links both national and international, and across Leicestershire so he persuaded the political leaders of the benefits of increasing the work of the Chairman and also spending more on hospitality.

Sam Jones left to become Town Clerk to the City of London where he served with distinction until 1997 when he 'retired'.

His successor was David Prince. He had to handle the aftermath of the enquiry into the Frank Beck affair and begin to frame the Councils response to the approaching Local Government Review, though he did leave with the reputation of having upset many of the District Councils and this, in the event, did not serve the County Council well as the review progressed. When David Prince left, the Authority did the sensible thing in my opinion and finally appointed John Sinnott who had been Sam Jones Deputy. John had to steer the County Council through the traumas of the massive change caused by the Local Government Review, which was a very painful process involving redundancies, enforced early retirements of valued colleagues and the breakdown of personal relationships. It was a very difficult time for the County Council and John Sinnott did an extremely professional job, the value of which may not be fully understood for some years.

John was Chief Executive when I was Chairman and I count myself very fortunate. He was a source of willing and valuable support and at the same time friendly and very down to earth.

The council also hosted the office of the Lord Lieutenant and the High Sherriff as well as a number of smaller services such as the County Records Office, the Registration service, the Coroners service and it also managed the County Farms Estate.

# Chapter Three
# CIVIC LIFE
## The Civic Team

I woke up on the morning of May 16th 1995 as the Chairman of the County Council for a year. It was a daunting prospect though, thankfully, there was a team of people at County Hall who supported the Chairman.

Leicestershire County Council was renowned for doing things properly as far as civic affairs were concerned and the reason for this is a professional team of officers and staff in the civic office and the other related services that the Chairman relies on to perform his duties properly. The civic office is located within the Chief Executives Department, who is also the Clerk to the Lieutenancy, and as such is responsible for organising the itinerary and arrangements for the Lord Lieutenant, the Queens representative in the County.

In Leicestershire for many years the Chief Executive had delegated all the day today administration of both the Lieutenancy and the Chairman to an Assistant Chief Executive and I was fortunate to have Bob Collins looking after me. After all he was the man mainly responsible for the high reputation that Leicestershire had, both for hospitality and for organisation. I realised very quickly that a well organised and knowledgeable civic office was absolutely critical to a Chairman being able to represent the County, able to relax and concentrate on the job in hand knowing that the arrangements were in order.

Throughout my year as Chairman Bob Collins was a much valued source of support and encouragement, always concerned to ensure that we were both well briefed, always checking to make sure that nothing could go wrong, and willing to offer advice. He also wrote the text whenever a speech was called for. Not that it was always used but Bob always made sure that the form was followed, there were things that needed to be said, names needed mentioning and people needed thanking. Bob made sure this was all taken care of.

Chairman and Lady
Leicestershire County Council

He was so meticulous that in readiness for the visit of the delegation from Kilkenny for instance, more of which later, he would keep his eyes open throughout the year for news items about Kilkenny, or Ireland so that the Chairman could draw on topical and humorous anecdotes in his speech at the welcoming dinner. He would also arrange for photocopies of the 'Who's Who' entry to be available whenever an important person had to be entertained. This was of great help, for instance, when I had to entertain Dr Laxmi Singvi, the Indian High Commissioner. His entry in *Who's Who* revealed that he was a Ghandi scholar and a poet. A valuable piece of information that helped to promote conversation and ensure that a guest was properly entertained.

Whatever the function we were always advised on dress and protocol, briefed about current topics of interest and offered some historical context for a foreign delegation for instance. I cannot recall an event or a function for which we were not properly briefed and therefore were never caught off guard. All this thoughtful planning and organisation made the Chairman and Lady feel very special, and therefore, more importantly, feeling in top form ready to represent the County with dignity and some style. It mattered! The thought of arriving at an important event wrongly dressed, not knowing what to say and, heaven forbid, probably late as well, is the civics nightmare.

When I was first elected to the council in 1975 the Chairman's car was a Rolls Royce, a lovely car although a hangover from the old days. It lasted until the politics changed in 1981, when the Conservatives lost control and the Council had no overall majority. I recall the debate when the decision was taken to sell the rolls. Labour members were unimpressed by Conservative claims that the car was needed to maintain the dignity and standing of the council. Conservatives pointed out that the City of Leicester, which was Labour controlled had its own Rolls-Royce, and indeed a distinctive number plate ABC 1. A Labour member suggested that if the chairman needed to be transported about a mini would suffice, it was a very functional motor car and very economical, there was no need for pomp and no need to put on a show.

The Chairman then was Bob Angrave but Mrs Janet Setchfield, a rather large lady, a senior Labour member and a former Lord Mayor of the City of Leicester was Vice Chairman and would become Chairman in May 1982. One Conservative speaker made the point that frequently ladies had to wear large hats for civic events and a car the size of a mini would be totally inappropriate. "I don't know whether Mrs Setchfield had ever tried it in the back of a mini," he said, meaning of course wearing a large hat, but too late he realised the unintended double meaning and watched helplessly as the council collapsed in mirth around him. The mental picture of Mrs Setchfield 'trying it' in the back of a mini had proved too much for all us and the debate ended with the council in fits of laughter and the decision to sell the Rolls Royce confirmed.

The saddest person when the Rolls was sold was Alan Clarke, the chauffeur, he loved that car and always felt it was the right car for a County Council chairman. Since then the Chairman's car has been a Daimler and also, since then, the Chairman's chauffeur has been Alan Clarke. He became Alan Clarke OBE in 1995, for services to Leicestershire. No one deserved this very special accolade more than Alan.

A modest genuine man, very likeable and determined to serve the Chairman and his beloved Leicestershire Alan was the epitome of the job specification, 'Chauffeur and Chairman's Attendant'.

And attend he did! Every Chairman would confirm that being looked after by Alan Clarke was something very special, every-

ALAN WITH THE CAR

thing about him was faultless, the way he dressed, the way he acted, the way he would reconnoitre each venue to ensure that the Chairman was not embarrassed by being put down in the wrong place, and where to park and all that. The car was always immaculate, I have known us to be out late at an official function one evening with an early start the next day and Alan Clarke would have been back in the garage in the early hours cleaning and polishing the car so that not a mark showed. In fact he was his own worst enemy because the car seemed never to show its age and the decision to replace it was always clouded in mystery because whatever their age Alan Clarke's cars always looked in tip top condition.

There are many, many examples of the professionalism of Alan Clarke, to him the Chairman and Lady were special, not as individuals but as representatives of the County of Leicestershire, and were looked after as such.

I recall three particular incidents that demonstrate his thoughtfulness and consideration. One of our first civic engagements was an outdoor military band concert organised in the grounds of Beaumanor Hall. We assembled during the afternoon amid warm summer sunshine and had tea and cakes. The band began to play and just as dusk started to fall the interval was taken. As the sun disappeared it suddenly felt cold and we began to shiver, Hilary said, "I'm beginning to feel cold, I wish we had brought a rug or something".

As if by magic Alan Clarke appeared, he could not have heard what she had said but in his hand was a rug that was soon wrapped around the Chairman's Lady, who then enjoyed the rest of the concert in comfort. Such thoughtfulness was typical of Alan Clarke. Another example was when we attended an evening musical event in St Mary De Castro church accompanied by the Lord Mayor and Lady Mayoress of Leicester. Whilst we were inside the weather had changed and as we approached the church door at the end of the programme we could hear the rain pounding on the roof. As the door was opened the teeming, pouring rain was evident. "Oh," said the Lady Mayoress, "you'd think the chauffeurs would be there with umbrellas wouldn't you."

"Well" said the Chairman's Lady "Ours is!" and there was Alan Clarke standing just outside the door waiting with large umbrella to escort us in comfort through the downpour to the car.

## Very Dignified and Very Alan Clarke!

And finally a Christmas carol concert at Enderby. As the service ended the civic party turned and made their way to the back of the hall for cups of tea and a mince pie. Half way there Hilary and I saw an old friend and stopped for a chat. As we finished our conversation our friend pointed to the tea table at the back of the hall and said "look at that queue you'll never get a cup of tea now". Then we saw Alan Clarke standing a discrete few yards away having got to the tea and mince pies first, a tray in hand with a cup of tea and a mince pie for each of us, we didn't have to queue at all. Not Alan Clarke's Chairman.

Oh yes, we were attended to very well by Alan Clarke!

I was looking forward to being 'looked after' by Alan Clarke and was somewhat dismayed to find out during our year as Vice Chairman that he was contemplating retirement. Thankfully he stayed on and though he was due to officially retire in the February of our year he sought permission to stay in his post until my year of office ended in May of 1996. We took this as a compliment and both Hilary and I were very pleased and we, and Alan and Norma Clarke 'went out' together at the end of our civic year.

Alan was chauffeur number one; the reserve chauffeur who stood in when Alan was on holiday or needed a rest was another lovely man, one who we came to be very fond of.

Whilst not being a trained chauffeur Harry Coleman was a very able deputy for Alan.

I had heard mainly from Duncan Lucas, a past Chairman, that Harry was prone to getting lost but that said more about Duncan than Harry. Duncan Lucas must have been a nightmare for anybody to drive around and we found Harry just as reliable as Alan. He may not have had the chauffeuring experience that Alan Clarke had had but was just as proud to be serving the Chairman and Leicestershire and anyway with Harry you got a bonus. He was a first class photographer, witnessed by his nick-name 'Flash Harry', and we have a huge collection of photo-graphs from functions and events the length and breadth of the County, thanks to Harry.

There is one other key member of the Chairman's team. County Hall had built a reputation over many years for not only doing things properly but for putting on dinners and receptions

RESERVE CHAUFFEUR HARRY COLEMAN. AKA FLASH HARRY

The Chairman's Team. L. to R.
Bob Collins, Gail Gerard (Press Officer), Richard Hopkins
Catering Manager) & Maria Dennis (Chairman's P.A.)

both large and small with a standard of cuisine, ambience and style unrivalled around the civic circuit. The credit for this is largely down to Richard Hopkins, the catering manager and his team of chefs and other staff who worked in the restaurant at County Hall.

We received, on behalf of the Council obviously, many, many letters of thanks during the year from guests who had sampled the hospitality at County Hall at one of the many dinners held there. The 'dining room' would be a committee room decorated with elegant table settings with flowers and the emblem of the Royal Leicestershire Regiment, 'The Tigers', a large silver tiger would be in place on the Chairman's table. The seating would have been given lots of thought so that guests found themselves sitting with interesting people and conversation flowed. The grace would be said usually by the Chief Executive and then a wonderful array of food, not necessarily expensive but cooked with imagination and with all the trimmings, good wine, red and white followed by port and cheese.

I cannot remember any occasion when Richards stilton was less than exquisite, the wines always carefully selected and served at just the right temperature and the port exceptional. All would be served quickly and efficiently with a smile and good humour. The whole evening would prove to be a memorable occasion and live in the memory. The Chairman got the credit but it was Richard and all his staff who consistently delivered excellence in every respect. The name that Leicestershire has for the quality of its hospitality is in no small measure down to Richard Hopkins.

## The Civic Programme

I had spent some time thinking about what the focus of this Chairman's year would be and I was determined to plan a strategy and stick to it.

There is no job specification for the office of Chairman. Obviously the Chairman must chair the meetings of the County Council, and by convention the Chairman withdraws from normal committee activity, and avoids political controversy so that the impartiality of the office can be maintained. There will be then be the conventional civic events, those that are fixed and happen every year, and those one off events such as Royal visits, when the Chairman represents the County of Leicestershire. Beyond that a Chairman can be high or low profile, and do as much or as little as he wants. I had made arrangements with my full time occupation so that I would be free to do just what I wanted 'in the office of Chairman.'

For this was not just any year. It was year critical to the future of the County Council, a year when Government would decide if the County Council would actually be abolished or at least have its powers so reduced that it would change beyond all recognition.

I had always felt that much of the work done by the various departments of the County Council was first class, and much of it went on largely without recognition. The Council had many gifted chief officers and staff who only wanted to provide good efficient services for the residents of the County. The ethos of 'the local government officer' though under threat from the drive to privatise and contract out services still provided the dominant motive for the staff of the County Council.

I decided that as Chairman I would do whatever I could to raise the profile of the County Council, the departments and the people who worked for it by visits and by actively seeking publicity for the work that the County Council did on behalf of the people of Leicestershire. There was much ignorance about what the council did and for what it was responsible that had led to the feeling that it was too big and too remote and it would be precisely this public attitude that would render the Council liable for reform by the Local Government Commission.

There are a number of 'permanent' civic dignitaries who we would meet on a regular basis at all kinds of events and functions. We had some experience during the year as Vice Chairman so had got to know the Lord Lieutenant, Tim Brookes and The Hon. Anne Brooks. We always enjoyed their company and they were both very supportive and helpful. I had known the former Lord Lieutenant Sir Andrew Martin, who was much loved and respected for the work he had done for young people. I guess taking over from him was a daunting task but as usual Leicestershire had found the ideal successors. Together the Brooke's soon stamped their own style and personality on the Lieutenancy and were a welcome sight at many of the events we were to attend during the year.

WITH THE LORD LIEUTENANT, TIM AND ANNE BROOKES

The High Sherriff and his wife too were very pleasant company, though their year changes half way through ours so we were able to get to know two incumbents. I still don't know how High Sherriff's are selected but obviously someone does and whoever does it and however it is done certainly works because both the High Sherriff's we got to know did a fine job for Leicestershire and were charming and helpful colleagues on the civic round.

John Whitehead was High Sherriff when I was first made Chairman, so as well as meeting often during our Vice Chairman's year I renewed an association that covered both business and the time we had spent on the Governing body of Leicester Polytechnic when John was Chairman and I was Vice Chairman for many years.

John was always so very well supported by his wife Alanda, who Hilary and I came to like enormously. Both John and Alanda helped us in many ways during our year by their obvious and unflagging support. However confident and self-assured I sometimes must have seemed it was so, so nice for someone to say 'well done, that went well' sometimes and that is the value of such good friends as John and Alanda. During the year they stepped down and Joe and Sarah Cowan took over. Once again Leicestershire were well served by two extremely gifted people both with a fine sense of public service, as well as a sense of humour so important if the burden of duty is to be lightened occasionally.

The role of the High Sherriff is closely linked to the legal system and it was Joe Cowan, who succeeded John Whitehead, who revised the tradition of having a service dedicated to the legal profession at the Cathedral. It was one of the best services I attended during the year and began by Joe reading an opening passage on the subject of law and civilised society in the context of democracy.

The civic year begins in May with the Annual General meeting of the County Council when the Chairman and Vice Chairman are elected, and so join the permanent civics for a year.

There are then meetings for normal Council business in June, September, November, January and March, with the very important budget meeting held in February, though in my year we had two budget meetings. I did have the opportunity to chair one meeting as Vice Chairman during the previous year. It was special meeting called to settle the very heated and important

JOHN (HIGH SHERRIFF) AND ALANDA WHITEHEAD,

issue of the sale of elderly persons homes because this was a one item council it was a very useful trial run for the full year as Chairman.

The first of the other fixed events that I had to be involved in was the Annual County Service. It is the Chairman who acts as the host for this event, which is one of the highlights of the civic year. The County Council is the senior local authority in the County and because it has links with the Lieutenancy and Shrievalty and the judiciary the County Service is almost an annual pageant, a spectacle when the life of the County in all its forms and at every level is on show. Invitations go out to representatives of the every walk of life across Leicestershire and I wanted to plan a memorable service around the theme of 'education and civilised society'.

The traditional venue for the service is Leicester Cathedral but the layout is not ideal and in any event I wanted to have the service as near to my patch as possible. If Stoney Stanton church had been big enough I would have held it there but it wasn't. The nearest suitable church, which could accommodate the huge congregation and also had a room for receiving the procession party and somewhere near enough for the post service reception was St. Mary's in Hinckley. It was chosen for just that reason because I had no idea when the decision was made what a splendid chap was in charge of St Mary's. I was about to find out as Bob Collins had arranged a meeting to plan the service with Brian Davies. He had done a wonderful job there since his appointment and had made a reputation for innovation and change that worried some no doubt but which was bringing more people into church and slowly improving the fabric. I had never seen a church with a coffee bar in the knave before but it seemed to work and more importantly set the church in a context with its surroundings. It wasn't separate and different but central to the locality it served.

We set out what we would wish to see, and set the general theme and made some suggestions about what hymns we would like. We suggested that we involve the choir from Manorfield School in Stoney Stanton and Brian liked the theme and suggested a flautist to perform, the involvement of the junior church and many other ideas. He suggested asking people from different walks of life to write and say their own prayers for the intercessions and slowly the pattern of what we all thought would be a fresh and different approach to the County service began to emerge.

We began to talk about what readings would be appropriate, because by tradition one lesson is read by the Chairman and one by the Lord Lieutenant, I had a problem. I was not a churchgoer and because of this I felt it not right for me to read from the bible. I suggested that I read from my favourite book of gentle philosophy and both Bob Collins and Brian Davies agreed.

I had first come across the Meditations of Marcus Aurelious in John Steinbecks East of Eden and had become very fond of it and turned to it whenever I felt in need of advice or guidance. I chose two fairly short passages to read. Marcus Aurelius was Emperor of Rome 121 to 180 AD and one of the first stoics, and in the context of his time considered to be a humanitarian ruler. The first passage I chose to read was from Book 3 Verse 5.

*"In your actions let there be a willing promptitude, yet a regard for the common interest; due deliberation, yet no irresolution; and in your sentiments no pretentious over-refinement. Avoid talkativeness, avoid officiousness. The God within you should preside over a being who is virile and mature, a statesman, and a ruler; one who has held his ground, like a soldier waiting for the signal to retire from life's battlefield and ready to welcome his*

*relief; a man whose credit need neither be sworn to by himself nor vouched by others. Therein is the secret of cheerfulness, of depending on no help from without and needing to crave from no man the boon of tranquillity. We have to stand upright ourselves, not be set up".*

AND second from Book 11 verse 21.

*"If a man's life has no consistent or uniform aim, it cannot itself remain consistent or uniform. Yet that statement does not go far enough unless you can also add something of what the aim should be. Now, it is not upon the whole range of things which are generally assumed to be good that we find uniformity of opinion to exist, but only upon things of a certain kind: namely those which affect the welfare of society. Accordingly, the aim we should propose for ourselves must be the benefit of our fellows and the community. Whoso directs his every effort to this will be imparting a uniformity to all his actions, and so will achieve consistency with himself".*

I thought it was to Brian Davies's credit that he offered no objection because although the passages themselves contained a Christian theme they had been written by a Roman whose countrymen had not taken to kindly, to say the least, to the idea of Christianity.!

The weather on the day was very mixed and as the procession party gathered a gentle rain started which took the edge away from the spectacle, but the service itself was as good as we had hoped it would be. The church was full, the hymns were sung with a gusto that warmed the heart, and Brian Davies delivered a fine sermon, bang on the theme of the service. Someone remarked later that it was not so much a church service but more like the Brian Davies show.

We had some letters of congratulations after the service; everyone who passed comment was very complimentary though I guess there would be some who might have preferred a more traditional form of service.

The other fixed civic event was the Chairman's reception at Beaumanor Hall.

Until just preceding the Second World War in 1939, the famous Herrick family owned the Beaumanor estate which consisted of Beaumanor Hall, several farms, St Mary's in the Elms church, the vicarage house, Garats Hay, workers houses and cottages along Forest Road and 350 acres of beautiful parkland.

After the war the Beaumanor estate passed back to Lt. Col. Assheton Penn Curzon Howe Herrick, who in 1946, for financial reasons decided to dispose of his assets. In a sale conducted at the Town Hall in Loughborough in December 1946, the War Department bought both Beaumanor Hall and Garat's Hay and some of the immediate surrounding grounds used during the war.

In the mid-1970s the hall was bought by the Leicestershire County Council, and it was quickly developed into a busy Conference and Education Centre.

It was also used for a number of events hosted by the Chairman, but the most notable was the Annual Beaumanor Reception held early in the new civic year, the intention being to allow the new Chairman to be introduced to a whole spectrum of people from business, commerce, voluntary and charity sector, the youth service, sport, the services and of course the other civic heads from Leicestershire and the neighbouring counties.

In my memory the event had been held at the home of the Chairman, which was fine when that was, say the Duke of

BEAUMANOR HALL

Rutland, so the venue was Belvoir Castle, but the changed nature of the office of Chairman meant that many Chairman were of modest means and with homes not large enough to cope with the necessary numbers of invited guests and so Beaumanor was selected as the permanent venue for the reception.

So that bookings could be made the date had been fixed before I was elected to the chair and because the pattern and style of the event is well established there is little a Chairman can do to stamp any personality or character on it. We did decide that brass band music outside would add a touch of magic and this had been arranged.

We could not have wished for a better weather, a warm balmy summer evening, good food, good wine, brass band music lots of friends. It was a great success in fact we were to be very lucky with weather all year, the only event slightly affected by adverse weather as I noted above was the County service.

The other fixed Civic events are the dinners at County Hall and those at Castle House which is used regularly by the Chairman of the County Council for entertaining.

Castle House has been in the ownership of the County Council since 1889 and is now maintained as lodgings for Her Majesty's High Court Judges who sit in Leicester, and for the entertainment of distinguished guests of the County Council by the Chairman of the Council. Castle House lies within a surprisingly quiet enclave near to the centre of the City and together with the Castle Hall, now known as 'The Castle', The Church of St. Mary de Castro and the Turret Gateway forms part of the ancient Leicester Castle.

Perhaps the Castles principle claim to fame is it's close association with Simon de Montfort, Earl of Leicester, whose leadership of the barons against Henry III in the middle of the thirteenth century is a matter of national rather than local history. The last Earl of Leicester to reside at Leicester Castle was John o' Gaunt whose death in 1399 marked the beginning of the crown's ownership of the castle through the Duchy of Lancaster. The Castle was the scene of the Parliament held in Leicester in 1425–1426.

Castle House itself is really three separate, though now connected buildings. The two timber framed buildings were erected following a fire in the middle of the fifteenth century. Very few domestic buildings of the fifteenth or sixteenth

centuries have survived in Leicester and therefore these buildings are of particular importance.

In 1974 Colonel P.H. Lloyd, at that time Chairman of the County Council, established the present custom, which is observed at luncheons and dinners, of the host saying the grace especially written for Castle House by the Lord Bishop of Leicester,

*Gracious O Lord are thy Gifts of Food and Drink;*
*Gracious too, this place where we enjoy them.*
*Let gratitude fill our lives with joy and*
*Equity our Land with Justice*
*Through Jesus Christ our Lord,*
*Amen*

I was to say this grace many times during the year and it was always especially poignant for me. I had known P.H. (Penn) Lloyd, who, though no longer Chairman was still a member of the County Council when I was elected in 1975. He was a lovely man and the fact that I was following in the footsteps of a man of such stature acted as an encouragement to me to perform the duties of Chairman with dignity.

During the course of each civic year Castle House is used to entertain other civic heads from the nine district councils in Leicestershire, another dinner to which are invited the Chairman, and Ladies of the neighbouring counties, Lincolnshire, Nottinghamshire, Derbyshire, Northamptonshire and Staffordshire, and an evening to dine with the other Leicestershire dignitaries, The Lord Lieutenant, the High Sherriff, The Bishop and the Chief Constable and the Chief Executive of the County Council.

These dinners are not costly, lavish affairs, and because Castle House is maintained as a judges lodging the costs of which are funded by the Home Office the only direct costs of the evening is the cost of the food, it's preparation and staff time. The House is full of history and character, it has a charm and an ambience that almost guarantees a memorable evening. Richard Hopkins and his staff are responsible for the food which was always of the highest quality. The Chairman is consulted about the menu and also the guest list. Dress is always black tie and there is always fourteen at table, if anyone drops out at the last minute there is a panic, because by tradition there must never be thirteen at table and we managed to preserve this tradition throughout the yea, but only just.

The guest list for the District Council dinners always followed a pattern, the civic head and Lady of the District Council being entertained, the Chief Executive and partner, and three County Councillors and partners of course, invited by the Chairman of the County Council, and who represent County council seats in the district whose Chairman and Chief executive are being entertained, and the Chief Executive of the County Council and partner.

There are also a series of regular dinners at County Hall, which as with Castle House are not costly or lavish affairs. The pattern is well established and I believe a welcome and much valued part of the county social and recreational life. There are evening dinners for the world of sport, the business world, the voluntary sector, representatives of education across the County and the ethnic minorities. The dinner for those service organisations having special links with the County is always a splendid affair as mess dress is the order of the evening and makes for a spectacle as well as a feast.

There are other dinners and receptions across the County that are regular features of a civic year. Each of the District Councils have their own civic events, some more formal than others, and the Chairman is invited to all of them as a representative of the County.

Just as the Chairman of Leicestershire invites the civic leaders of our neighbouring counties to a number of events in Leicestershire, so they invite the Chairman of Leicestershire to civic events in their county. It is this exchange of mutual hospitality that brings opportunities to get to know colleague civics very well.

The term 'chain gang' is often used to describe the collection of the civics that meet on so many civic occasions during any one year. It is not a term I have used, nor one that I like, but we did get to know a number of people who held civic office alongside us over the two years we were involved.

I shared a number of occasions with Harry Lowe, the genial and genuine, Labour Chairman of Derbyshire, Reg Strauther Chairman of Nottinghamshire and also got to know the long serving, almost legendary Chairman of Staffordshire, John O'Leary. Naturally we shared many civic events with the Lord Mayor and Lady Mayoress of the City of Leicester but we came to like and enjoy the company of all the other civic heads right across the County, and not forgetting Rutland of course.

There are certain rules that are quickly learnt, and here the established 'professional dignitaries' are a real help.

The civic heads who we came to know well during the year are listed in alphabetical order.

**Chairman of Blaby**
Councillor F.E. Spence & Mrs Spence
(Fred and Hazel)

**Mayor of Charnwood Councillor**
J.E. Hawkes & Mrs Hawkes
(John and Lyn)

**Chairman of Harborough Councillor**
E. Hubbard & Mrs Hubbard
(Eric and Joyce)

**Mayor of Hinckley & Bosworth**
Councillor Mrs J. Crooks & Mr Crooks
(Joyce and Bill)

**Lord Mayor of the City of Leicester**
Councillor M. Johnson and Mrs Johnson
(Mike and Marion)

**Mayor of Melton**
Councillor T.E. Netherton & Mrs Netherton.
(Tom and Joyce.)

**Chairman of North West Leicestershire**
Councillor T.A. Smith and Mrs Smith
(Alfie and Pam)

**Mayor of Oadby and Wigston**
Councillor Mrs S.A. Spence and Mrs A. Bee
(Shirley and Amanda)

**Chairman of Councillor Rutland**
B.A. Montgomery & Mrs Montgomery
(Brian and Pam)

Though each civic year follows, in the main, a familiar and well known routine, each year is different because of the interests of the personalities involved and also because each year brings different anniversaries and historical features.

The civic year 1995/6 was just such a year. It was the 50th Anniversary of VJ day, it was the 350th anniversary of the battle of Naseby and the events that marked the turning point in the English Civil War, it was also the 40th Anniversary of the Duke of Edinburghs Award Scheme, and many other similar events that needed to be marked and celebrated.

There were the Royal Visits, Princess Anne made three visits to Leicestershire in that year and we went to Buckingham

PRESENTING H.R.H. WITH A COPY OF THE RURAL STRATEGY

Palace and St. James Palace, and there was an historic first visit to Leicestershire by The Lord Mayor of London.

There were many overseas visitors and of course our own visits abroad. We met many people who would be considered important, Cabinet Ministers, Ambassadors, Peers of the Realm and others, and those who might not be considered important, but who often turned out to be more important in their own right, and who we enjoyed meeting just as much.

We made friends with many people both here and overseas and I got to know a lot more about this wonderful County of ours, not just in the context of the work of the County Council but its personalities, its institutions both statutory and voluntary from east to west and north to south. There were many events that were planned and organised by departments of the County Council and some that I personally planned and carried out.

One event in particular that I was determined to introduce onto the County Hall dinner agenda was one to recognise the contribution made by so many unsung hero's of this County, the many people who made a personal commitment to serving their local community either as a Parish, District or County Councillor. It

LORD (CHRISTOPHER WALFORD) AND LADY MAYORESS OF LONDON

seemed to me that if it was right for the County Council to recognise the contribution to the life of our County made by sportsmen or educationalists or ethnic minorities then it was just as important to recognise that special group of people who served largely without remuneration or recognition the areas in which they lived, some of whom had served for most of a lifetime.

I had also promised to do whatever I could to support the work of the Sir Andrew Martin Trust. If it had been possible I would have used the office of Chairman to raise funds for the trust in the same way that some Mayors and Chairman of district councils select a charity to support during their year of office.

However it was pointed out that there is no tradition of the Chairman of the County Council having a charity, an argument that did not impress me, but it was true that if the full weight of the County Council and it's departments were to be committed to a Chairman's charity for the civic year then it would seriously affect the charity work of the other district civic leaders. This did make some sense so I did not protest too much. But I was determined to do something, after all Sir Andrew's family had been very prominent in County affairs and his uncle was a former distinguished Chairman of the County Council!

I had known Sir Andrew when he was Lord Lieutenant, our paths often crossed, mainly because we shared an interest in youth work and the welfare of young people and I had used an occasion when we played in the same cricket team, by way of an anecdote at the launch of the trust, to illustrate his ability to get on with young people. The trust which carries his name will raise funds, which will be invested so that the income that is generated can be used to help young people. It was so very appropriate because he had a genuine concern for the welfare of young people and, surprisingly for a man of his station, he had a remarkable ability to talk to and communicate with young people from every walk of life. I recall many examples of his enthusiasm for and interest in young people. I recall him in animated conversation with a group of youths all with brightly coloured Mohican haircuts at a Duke of Edinburgh's Award event at Stafford I think it was. It was a memorable scene, he in his official uniform, tall and elegant with a white military mous-

WITH MR & MRS GEORGE MARRIOTT.
LONG SERVING PARISH COUNCILLOR IN STONEY STANTON

WITH NEVILLE AND MRS SMITH. LONG-SERVING MEMBER OF SAPCOTE PARISH COUNCIL

tache, and the young people with the strange haircuts and jeans with safety pins stuck all over them.

I also recall a cricket match in which I and my son Paul played. It was a County Hall team in which Sir Andrew always played in the odd friendly match. Paul who was only about fourteen at the time took a turn at bowling and I watched as between overs Sir Andrew offered him coaching in how to make the ball swing and on one delivery where Paul succeeded in bowling an absoluter corker of an out swinger, Sir Andrew, who was keeping wicket, took the catch. Sir Andrew danced down the pitch in delight and gripped a somewhat bewildered Paul by the hand. I have never forgotten that. Sir Andrew was genuinely and utterly delighted and for me this was a man who enjoyed the company of young people, shared their aspirations and rejoiced in their successes and cared about the world they lived in. There were no cameras around, no photographers, no microphones and so there was no element of putting it on, no suggestion that this was a performance for effect only, this was the real Sir Andrew Martin, a man I had so much respect for, that to be able to do anything to support a trust that carries his name, and which would be used to support young people, was a pure and absolute pleasure.

One of the first things for the trust was actually a suggestion of Bob Collins, which was readily agreed to by Brian Davies and it was that half the collection at the county service would go into the funds of the trust and the other half would go towards the refurbishment fund at St Marys Church. An extremely appropriate arrangement given that the theme of the County service was education and civilised society.

I also persuaded some long standing business colleagues to make donations which helped swell the total. But I wanted to do more and once again Bob Collins came up with a suggestion and set about devising a scheme which would involve the youth organisations, a project he was calling the Chairman's Journey across Leicestershire and sponsorship and competitions that would raise money for the trust and involve the chairman in visiting the many and varied county council facilities and schemes all across Leicestershire and Rutland. Planning for this event, involved talking to the various County Hall departments so that the journey could be arranged to bring some attention to the work that goes on sometimes in far flung locations that are of benefit to Leicestershire people.

In the event it was this planning that eventually revealed that the effort and indeed the cost of planning and executing the journey would not be reflected in the amount of money raised and so the idea was not pursued.

The idea however did manifest itself later in the civic year as the Chairman's journey of fun in April and was so very worthwhile but not as a fundraiser for the Trust. I had to think about something else for that and I eventually put an idea to Bob Collins that took him by surprise, though to his credit he listened carefully and though he was obviously doubtful to begin with he did set about making it possible.

I had always been impressed by the way 'bikers', those black leather clad men and women who rode the strange and distinctive long and high handled bared motor bikes, could raise money for charity and so belie their public image of being a bit scruffy and not very law abiding. I had always enjoyed a days fishing and knew that the angling fraternity were of a similar breed to the bikers. Passionate about their pastime, naturally generous and gregarious and able, when they set their minds to it, to raise money for a good cause.

The project came to fruition and a match was held at King Lears Lake at Watermead Country Park thanks to help from lots of people, including the County Fire service, Roy Marlow who ran a local fishery and tackle shop and lots of others.

## Overseas Links

The County Council has educational links with The Saarland, in Germany, Seine Maritime in France, and Florence in Italy and a long standing, though whilst I was Chairman an unofficial, twinning arrangement with Kilkenny in the Irish Republic. Before I had been elected Chairman there was already a trip to Saarbrucken in the Diary. April 1996 was the date of the Saarmesse, a major international exhibition and trade fair in Saarbrucken and Leicestershire was to celebrate 25 years of the twinning arrangement by linking with the Leicestershire Chamber of Commerce and Industry and taking a stand at the exhibition and in being invited to the opening ceremony. The Leicestershire Schools Big Band, and the Youth Dance group were to perform at the opening and play at the exhibition during a Sunday lunchtime live radio broadcast on Saarland Radio.

I also expressed a wish to give the link with Florence some attention because it was a link that was in danger of failing because of the cost of getting school children to Florence. Schools could drive to Saarland and Seine Maritime at a cost acceptable to parents but to get to Florence really meant a journey by air. Yet Florence was such an important place for the proper understanding of European history, art history in particular, and I wanted to make sure that our colleagues in Florence were assured that we valued the link and wanted it to endure.

During the summer of 1995 I fulfilled one or two engagements in cooperation with the County Cricket Club, who managed the Mini cricket programme on behalf of the County Council. There was also a long standing association between the Club and the County Council through the schools coaching system. I came to know and very much admire the work that the club did in coaching and developing the junior players. Russell Cobb in particular was doing a tremendous job all across the County. Largely through the contacts that Russell had built up in South

Africa, Leicestershire Young Cricketers had formed a friendly association with the Wanderers Club in Johannesburg which meant that every two years a team of under 19s visited South Africa and the following year a team of under 19s from the Wanderers visited Leicestershire. The Under 19s were due to play a series of matches in Johannesburg and Eastern Transvaal during late December 1995 and early January 1996.

The Club invited the Chairman to join the party and support the tour by attending some of their matches in South Africa, and it was decided that subject to other civic and goodwill elements being included that it would be appropriate particularly given the political situation in South Africa that such a trip might be useful too in establishing some business and commercial links in the emerging economic revival of the newly constituted republic. It was purely coincidental that at the same time a full England cricket team would be touring South Africa and that the itinerary was to be constructed so as to enable us to see at least two of the one day internationals!

The Kilkenny link was a regular and permanent fixture in the Chairman's diary and the visits had acquired folklore of their own and invitations to join the party were much sought after. The pattern had been established under the Chairmanship of Martin Ryan; it seems that news of the election of Martin, a native of Thomastown in County Kilkenny, to the Chairmanship of Leicestershire County Council, reached the ears of the Chairman of Kilkenny County Council, who was a relative of Martins and who naturally invited Martin over for a visit. The visiting Leicestershire party naturally issued a return invitation to the Chairman of Kilkenny County Council and so a tradition started and each year under different Chairman a Leicestershire delegation visits Kilkenny and a Kilkenny delegation visits Leicestershire. I had never been involved in way shape or form with these visits before I became Vice Chairman but every councillor knew what a delight it was to be in the company of 'the Irish', and some good times were talked about and so I had very much looked forward to both their visit to us and our return visit to Ireland.

So by the middle of November we had our travel arrangements well and truly mapped out, all our trips would take place in the later stages of our civic year starting very early in the new year when we would fly out to South Africa for ten days, then spend four days in Florence in early March, a long weekend in

Saarland in April and then the return trip to Kilkenny in May.

In addition to our trips abroad we would meet and greet a number of individuals and delegations from a whole variety of Countries at County Hall and elsewhere during our civic year. Turkish librarians, Cuban financial experts, a Sri Lankan business delegation, Japanese businessmen, scouts and local government trainees, Swiss special needs teachers, German educationalists, a group from France twinned with Enderby, the High Commissioner of India, Egyptian highway engineers, a youth drama group from Columbus Ohio USA, a group of Youth Workers from all over the continent, a twinning ceremony involving Broughton Astley and Geveze in France, a group of students and their teachers from Kiev who were visiting Babington Community College.

The Kilkenny delegation arrived in Leicester on 27th October and after a tour of the City I hosted a dinner at County Hall in their honour. It was the beginning of a very hectic four days; each day was different though including full lunch and dinner each day which made the enduring memory one of having over eaten. On the Saturday afternoon we had invited the delegation to Welford Road for lunch and then to watch the Tigers play Bristol. It was an exhilarating afternoon a memorable match with three of the best tries I have ever seen, one was to be voted the try of the season, and John Liley kicked a record number of points as Tigers not only won, but in reality thrashed Bristol.

When John Liley kicked one of the penalties the ball had sailed high and handsome through the posts and hit Martin Ryan, the leader of the Labour Group, on the nose, dislodging his spectacles and drawing blood. By sheer coincidence I had invited the Rugby Club to County Hall on the following Monday night for a reception in recognition of their success the previous year when they won the Division one championship. It seemed very appropriate therefore that, as this was the last evening of the Kilkenny trip that our Irish guests should join in the celebrations. It was a very successful evening. I did suggest to John Liley that to be fair he ought to let Martin Ryan kick a rugby ball at him but then thinking about it Martin might have done himself more damage than the ball had done when it hit him, so as there was a very remote possibility that Martin would hit anything anyway, never mind John Liley, the idea was dropped.

WITH THE TIGERS CAPTAIN, PAUL DODGE

We had got on very well with the Kilkenny people, some of whom knew Leicestershire well. Despite the problems with violence in Northern Ireland the atmosphere was very friendly and there was not a hint that the problems in the north could ever dent the strong friendship that had been built up over the years between Leicestershire and Kilkenny. Therein lies the value of such links, people from the two islands meet and talk and get to know each other and from that comes understanding and mutual respect and trust. We began to look forward to May 1996 when we would visit Kilkenny.

The trip to South Africa was a real adventure, and for me an opportunity to assess how the post apartheid system was working. We flew to Johannesburg on the third of January and arrived very tired and jet lagged but after a short rest we joined the under 19s cricket team that afternoon who were playing a match against Parktown Boys, which in the event was abandoned when a violent thunderstorm and massive downpour made cricket impossible.

The following day we drove to Ermelo in East Transvaal where we were well looked after by Peter and Elmarie Celliers, who were old friends of Russell Cobb. They were charming and generous hosts, farmers and business people, one of Peters interests was a construction and landscaping company and this Peter had used to construct a full size cricket pitch on his game reserve, which he had called Phumula Game Reserve, miles from anywhere, and converted some old farm buildings into dormitories for the visiting players and their families. We had noticed on our itinerary that no hotels had been booked for us in Ermelo, the programme read 'accommodation to be arranged', and we were about to find out why.

The dormitories were full, the Celliers own house was full and the nearest hotel was in Ermelo nearly an hour away by car, but we were told the zulu hut was free if we were prepared to stay in it. Zulu hut sounded exciting but this was Africa, where is it we asked, to be told it was down by the lake. Would you like to see it before you decide we were asked. Fine we said and we followed Peter and Elmarie as they drove their jeep around the farm buildings that were the dormitory, through a small wooded copse and along a track through a field and away from the farm. About half a mile away they stopped outside what appeared to

THE ZULU HUT IN ERMELO, SOUTH AFRICA

be a large half coconut turned upside down, sitting on a veranda right over the side of a lake. The silence was deafening, the birds were brightly coloured and the fields all around were alive with wildebeest, zebra, impala and ostrich on the ridge of the hill about a mile away. Hilary and I looked at each other as Elmarie opened the door.

It was small and low and African murals formed a line almost like sentries on the wall just before the door, which made it seem scary and added to the sense of mystery about the place. We had to duck very low to get into the hut which was very dark, with animal skins both on the floor and the walls and the bedcover was a magnificent zebra skin. It was cool, and it was clean and joy of joys there was a bathroom, with a proper toilet, and shower through a door at the back with hot water heated by liquid petroleum gas. And it was quiet, very quiet I have never before been to a place as quiet. Still it was then early afternoon and rather than appear to be whimps, we said this would be fine, and anyway we didn't fancy driving to and from a hotel in Ermelo morning and evening.

We dropped our cases and drove back to the farm and dormitories where a barbecue was being prepared for supper. It was truly wonderful, darkness falls quickly under African skies and we ate a memorable, if basic and simple meal, all gathered in the open around a large open fire burning with large logs of wood, before thinking about returning to the zulu hut.

Now, in the afternoon sun the hut had seemed almost a romantic and idyllic place, but in pitch darkness it assumed an almost sinister and menacing appearance. Even the short drive down to the lake was an eerie experience. It was pitch black and I could not get out of my mind that this was Africa, and that there were wild animals about which I thought would all wander down to the lake to drink when it got dark.

I parked the car as near to the hut as possible and left the headlights on so that we could see our way to get through the door of the hut and get the light on inside. This done I returned to the car to put the lights out and lock it up, though why I really don't know why for there would be no other person anywhere near. I was about to lock the car door when a muted squeal came from inside the hut and I rushed back in to find Hilary standing over the bed looking very scared and pointing in horror at something on the sheet.

It was long thin black thing with spiky antennae and hairs protruding from each end, it looked absolutely ghastly and very unpleasant. I grabbed the first thing that came to hand, which was a wooden plate, an ornament from the bedside table and cracked the thing over its back. It was obvious from the lack of reaction that it had not been alive and closer, though very careful examination revealed that it was nothing more than a long black twig which had obviously fallen out of the thatch overhead.

That was to set the tone for the night. Neither of us slept a wink, every noise, and there were many, seemed to be just outside the door or just above our heads. The hut was built on stilts over the edge of the lake so that almost directly underneath us there were hundreds of frogs, not croaking as our friendly English frogs would do, but screeching and yelling in all kinds of ways guaranteed to keep you awake all night wondering where the next noise would come from. And so at 4.30 the next morning I got up and ventured outside and how glad I am that I did. It was warm, the early morning sun quickly gains heat and all along the lake were brightly coloured birds, flashes of the brightest yellows and oranges you could imagine. Zebra and impala were roaming well within sight and a flock, if that is the right collective word, of ostrich waggled ungainly across the field a few hundred yards away. I sat in one of the chairs on the veranda and looked and let the tranquillity of the place overtake me this was Africa my first visit and it was special, so very special.

We made our way back up to the house where the dormitories were, and where after breakfast, the cricket match would begin. It was not a good match for the Under 19's. Something had given them all a bad stomach and the culprit was probably the burghers they all ate on the way to Ermelo the previous day.

There were barely enough of them fit enough to play! Unexpectedly it turned into a two day two innings each match they were really made to suffer in the searing heat. The match turned into something of an ordeal and the strong team spirit that had been built up was really put to the test. However it was a testament to the guidance and coaching of Colin Root and Russell Cobb that the players did not disgrace themselves and though they lost the match all the players, well led by Team Captain Neal Pullen, performed well.

We had to leave on the following morning Sunday the 7th Jan to drive back to Johannesburg and prepare for a flight to Cape Town the following morning.

Compared to Johannesburg, Cape Town seemed to be in a different country, which is not so surprising given the history of how South Africa was settled. Cape Town was the major entry port for the new continent and so was much more cosmopolitan, it had also been the place that the Boers had left to trek north all those years ago so it had retained more Englishness than any other place in South Africa.

We spent three days in Cape Town though we were not able to visit table mountain nor indeed see the cape itself partly to do with the weather but also because we were so well hosted that we had little free time. We had a civic meeting with the Mayor of Cape Town, a charming man and heard a lovely story, alleged to be true, about him. It seems that because the ceremony to install Nelson Mandella as president took place in Cape Town the Mayor was the civic host. Now this must have been one of the biggest state occasions anywhere in the world. Almost the totality of the worlds political and state heads were in attendance and the celebrations lasted for days.

Her Majesty the Queen had arrived in the Royal Yacht and a glittering reception was held to which this gathering of the world's most important people were invited. Think of it, South Africa's majority had triumphed after decades of struggle, a black man was president, the world and his wife had come to witness the festivities at this world shattering event.

WITH ANDREW BANTHAM, THE FIRST BLACK MAYOR OF CAPE TOWN

The Mayor of Cape Town greets the Queen, I quote what was reported in a local magazine, The Queen "Mr Mayor, don't you have a chain of office?" The Mayor replied "Why, yes M'am". The Queen "Then why aren't you wearing it?" The Mayor "I only wear it for special occasions." A lovely story. He meant to say civic occasions obviously!

We were also to meet a group of people who had a contract for distance learning with Leicester University and a cocktail party had been arranged in the evening. The following day was a joy. We were collected by Bill Henderson, one of the people involved and looked after like royalty all day. A sightseeing tour of the vineyards around Stellenbosch and a drive all along the coast at Fishoek and Windhoek revealed a coastline similar to the Amalfi coast near Naples and was very, very beautiful.

Finally, after a civic reception by the Mayor of Cape Town and lunch, a real treat with the rest of the day to watch a one day international cricket match between South Africa and England at Newlands, one of the worlds most famous grounds and reputed to be one of the most beautiful. Set around lots of trees with table mountain as a backdrop I could see why.

It was to be a day/night match starting at 3.00pm and going on until very late evening. It was so, so hot to begin with but when the sun went down it was warm and comfortable and very enjoyable. England looked like winning, they were on top all day, so the English fans were teasing the South African crowd and then in only the last 20 or 30 minutes England just threw the match away. They could have got the remaining runs required to win in ones and twos but tried to hit boundaries and one very injudicious stroke by Graham Thorpe, through which he lost his wicket, brought a collapse and left the many England supporters very disappointed, and the South African fans cock a hoop.

We had to be up early the next morning to return to Johannesburg.

Bill Henderson had looked after us really well in Cape Town and so it was a pleasure to be able to return the compliment when Bill and his wife paid a visit to Leicestershire that following March and April.

We had a number of official engagements in Johannesburg, which like the rest of South Africa, was experiencing a re-organisation of local government very similar to what has happening back home in the UK, though it seemed to me the South African Government were taking a more sensible approach.

I found it fascinating to talk to elected local politicians and council officers about the way the 'new' South Africa was changing. One thing that did seem sensible to me was the adoption of a 'dual' election system which meant that two thirds of the new council seats were decided by the first past the post system and one third by proportional representation. This was because it was obvious that in most areas by a simple first past the post system all the seats would go to the ANC and the national party would have no representation at all. The one third elected by PR would be allocated on the party list system which meant that each party knew which of their candidates would get elected which avoided the elimination of many experienced councillors and avoided a complete change bringing in many inexperienced members.

Given the history of oppression and violence that the ANC had suffered this seemed to me to be magnanimous and sensible gesture, indicating that the ANC were not adopting a policy of 'we are the masters now' and had the good sense to see that excluding the white minority from involvement in local, and indeed national government might backfire and lead to civil unrest. Very sensible and signalled to me a willingness to make a success of the new South Africa

It was extremely interesting to discuss the politics of the new South Africa with a number of senior officers and local politicians. We met the leaders of Johannesburg Metropolitan Council, Sandton District Council and Randburg Municipality.

The contacts made and the interest shown by Leicestershire might, for all we know, result in positive benefits for the economic well being of both South Africa and Leicestershire. There have already been serious discussions about exports to South Africa between industrialists in East Transvaal and business's in Leicestershire arising directly out of the visit we made, though no substantive developments have yet emerged.

It was also economic matters that were the prime reason for the visit to the Saarland, much work had already been done in planning the best way to celebrate the anniversary of the educational link. Our friends in the Saarland were very keen to broaden this educational link by developing economic, cultural and academic cooperation involving the universities in Leicestershire and Saarland.

I had met Herr Joachim Kiefaber earlier in the year when he came to Leicestershire to finalise arrangements for Leicestershire's involvement in the Saarmesse trade fair and the role the Chairman might play at the opening ceremony and in encouraging the Chamber of Commerce and Industry to persuade business's to take space. He also wanted to visit Snibston Discovery Park because Saarland had a proposal to turn a redundant steel works they had into a European Science Park.

The visit to Florence took place over a very cold weekend in the first few days of March and we had the added pleasure of being in the company of a school party from John Fernely High School in Melton who had the Headteacher Chris Robinson in charge. Chris and his school had been staunch supporters of the Leicestershire-Florence link for many years.

The visit did what was intended in demonstrating to our partners in Florence that we believed the link to be valuable and wanted to maintain and develop it as circumstances permitted. We had to acknowledge however that changes to the way educa-

WITH HERR GENSCHER. HE TOASTED THE UK, I TOASTED GERMANY.

tion is funded makes it very difficult for an LEA to nurture and develop these links which I believe to be an important element in the totality of the experiences that should be on offer to our young people.

The final 'foreign' trip of the civic year was the return visit to Kilkenny which took place during the first weekend in May. It was easy to understand why 'the Irish' have such a reputation for hospitality and friendship which only served to emphasise how much the conflict in the north had deprived the people on both sides of the Irish Sea of a fruitful and productive friendly relationship for most of this century. We were well looked after as we sent the first afternoon in Dublin at the magnificent Archeological Museum, then travelled, in a minibus to Kilkenny for a dinner at an Italian Restaurant in the evening.

Visits during the following day to places of historical interest around Kilkenny, and they are many gave us an interesting day. The Saturday evening saw us meeting the Mayor of Kilkenny City and joining him for dinner in the evening in a restaurant in Kilkenny. The real delight of the evening was after the dinner in a side room reserved for our party a duo of two young ladies playing Irish Harps entertained us with some lovely enchanting music which was a joy and pleasure to listen to. When the harpists left our hosts all did their party pieces but I have to say that the Leicestershire party did not do their share.!

So the following morning we bought some song books and learned the words so that on the Sunday evening we most certainly did hold our own and the duet of Danny Boy by Jean Lucas and Hilary was much appreciated, so much so that a hat was laid in the middle of the room and coins were thrown into it. The pile of coins grew even higher when the Chairman and Duncan Lucas attempted to dance an Irish Jig in the middle of the room. It was an evening to remember and, as I have said elsewhere in some small way, acts to repair the damage caused to Anglo-Irish relationships that have suffered so much for many years for obvious reasons.

## The Routine of Civic Life

Each week there would be the diary of engagements that enabled the proper planning of travel arrangements and dress and so on. This was important as it enabled us to mix and match our private life with civic duty. Each week there would be correspondence to deal with, invitations to open things, attend things, present things, say a few words at and event and altogether it amounted to a wonderful variety of daily visits and a mountain of preparation not to mention attention to dress and protocol.

We made a number of visits to schools and educational establishments, in all parts of the service and across all of the County. Sometimes I would be greeted by a group of pupils and shown around the school and these were always extra special visits. Mostly I would be shown around a head and introduced to staff in the classrooms and in this way I came to understand a lot more about how schools worked and about the pressures on staff and resources that were the main topic of conversation wherever I went. I was genuinely interested in making sure that heads and governors knew that the education authority was still keen to offer a lead, offer some vision and leadership to the family of schools across Leicestershire.

Everywhere I found dedicated teaching and support staff coping with massive change and under funding under the glare of the headlights of the media. Seemingly in spite of all the attention and change getting on the job of educating the young people of Leicestershire in as professional way as possible. I met some gifted head teachers who were in charge of some excellent schools both inside the City and across the County. I would not say that those I visited are better than any others because those I chose to visit were selected at random, and because of geographical location, but would say that they were representative of the general quality of schools in Leicestershire.

Over the two years of being Vice-Chairman and Chairman I must have visited 80 or so schools so I talked to a lot of teachers and head teachers and so gained a wide knowledge of how things were in the education world. Everywhere members of staff worked hard and were doing their best for the children in their care but often in poor conditions for teaching and learning with high class numbers and little or no support for those children needing special attention.

There were a number of openings when it was my privilege to share a special day with staff and pupils, anniversary celebrations and most enjoyably Christmas and other festivals all of which we both enjoyed enormously. There were also a number of excellent occasions when we could share the pleasure of watching children perform in every genre of artistic discipline from music to singing dance and drama which was proof positive of the quality of the Leicestershire system of music, dance and drama tuition.

I recall a very happy morning spent at Mayflower Primary in the City of Leicester. They were celebrating re-opening after refurbishment and I was invited to join the Chairman of Governors Geoff Rawnsley, a colleague County Councillor and the Head teacher Mrs Susan Nash. It is a very friendly school the children are open and alert, interested and talkative. I enjoyed my time there, cutting a cake with the Mayflower emblem and declaring the school open. Much to my delight I was invited back to the school late on in my year to bury a time capsule and once again had a wonderful time with all the children joining in.

The re-organisation of the special schooling system across the County meant that I was invited to join in the celebrations of the opening of Piper Way special school and also join in the sponsored walk around the school site, and also to join with Gary Lineker to re open the refurbished Ellesmere College.

It turned out that he and I were born quite close to each other in Braunstone, both attended Caldecote Road Primary school and the City of Leicester School. There the similarity ends, though I understand that he was once told to spend more time on his academic studies as he would 'get nowhere playing football' and I once had one teacher write on my report that 'If he put as much energy into his school work as he does into his sport he would make better progress.' In my case at least that was good advice!

One very enjoyable visit was to a small village school in Swinford near Lutterworth. The Headteacher was June Clayton and I had been to the school before to talk to the children and show some slides about the visit to India I had made some years before. It was obvious that the children were bright and bubbly and not at all afraid to engage in conversation. I had also opened the school fete at the very beginning of my term as Chairman so I knew that the school was well supported by parents and by the village in general and it was no surprise when in 1997 the school received an outstanding report from Ofsted. Well deserved and a credit to everyone connected with Swinford School.

AT SWINFORD SCHOOL WITH HEADTEACHER JUNE CLAYTON AND PUPILS.

I was also privileged to be asked to re-open the new Uplands Junior School after its rebuilding following a fire. We were well entertained by the pupils who performed an incredibly effective piece of drama and I handed the keys over to the Chairman of Governors Mr Ayub Zamadka.

After one visit to Hazel Street, where we met the Headteacher Pat Clarke and all the staff, Hilary and I were invited to join the school for their Christmas multi cultural lunch. This was a really joyous occasion when the whole school gathered together, pupils, teachers and governors for a menu that reflected the nationalities that made up this very culturally diverse and happy school.

Finally I cannot praise too much the people who run the School of Music, Dance and Drama. The way this service had evolved and acquired such a high national reputation is due to many people not least the parents of the students who had continually been asked not only to pay more but who also had to transport their children to and from rehearsals and performances. There were so many occasions when the sheer quality of the performances stayed in the memory. There were the concerts at De Montfort Hall where the singing and the music would ensure a quality musical evening.

The Youth Modern Dance Group won an award at the Edinburgh Festival and when they returned, they repeated the performance before a selected audience at The Lansdowne Centre. The Brass Band that played at Beaumanor on the occasion of the Chairman's evening was also from the School of Music.

I shall never forget either when we were in Saarbrucken, celebrating the 25th Anniversary of the official education link between the County Council and the Saarland, and we attended the official opening of the Saarmesse, a business fair, when, as we approached the doors to the entrance hall of the Saarbrucker Schloss the Leicestershire Schools Orchestra struck up and played all the delegates into the building and then young students from the School of Dance performed in the imposing main hall as Her Diedrich Gensher, the distinguished German politician, performed the official opening.

The dancers and the orchestra were also present on the Sunday when Radio Saarland broadcast an hour at lunchtime devoted to the anniversary of the link between Leicestershire and Saarland. Watching these talented young people, dancers and instrumentalists representing Leicestershire with such distinction brought a lump to my throat and, yes I admit it, a tear to my eye. They were magnificent!

On one day towards the end of the year I decided that I would indulge myself and make a civic visit to the three schools that I attended as a boy. Firstly Caldecote Road Junior School which I attended for a brief time when I was boarded out by my parents and stayed with my Grandmother while Mother got on with producing my youngest brother. I was only there for about three months.

My real primary school was Knighton Fields Road where I started as a three year old in the nursery, and stayed all through the infant school which was on one side of the large hall and then into the junior school on the other, and which I enjoyed mostly. It seemed very strange standing in the very room where I had played in the nursery as a three year old and looked out of the window where the climbing frames and the paddling pool used to be.

It also seemed to me that the hall, where I made my stage debut as King Herod in a school nativity play when I was eight, seemed to have shrunk somewhat! To a five year old it was a huge great hall.

I sat talking to the Head in his office wearing the civic regalia around my neck, the same office in which I sat the 11 plus exam all those years ago.

I could not visit the Grammar School I attended because it had been amalgamated and moved out of the City to a site along Downing Drive. The school I attended had been in a building in Humberstone Gate and is now the Age Concern Headquarters. It is a wonderful building and I always thought it was a perfect for a school, full of character, with stone staircases and a huge hall, that we called 'big school' and in which was full sized pipe organ that was always played in assembly by 'Bill' Sykes, a teacher who taught music, maths and French.

So when I made my civic visit I looked around the ' new' City of Leicester School I told the principal, Mr Lewis, that I was an old boy and this brought some added interest to my visit. As I walked around the school with three of the pupils he went into the vaults to look for any records of my time at the school. I enjoyed my visit and found at least one of the honours boards, large wooden boards that used to adorn the walls in 'big school' and on which were recorded the destinations and academic achievements of those pupils who made it to university. I returned to the principal's office to find that he had emerged from the vaults with my registration card from September 1952, and that, he said, was all he could find as there appeared to be no other records of my time at the school. I was not sorry! I had not been a model student and though I did work hard I had never been a bright pupil, nor always the best behaved.

However I had forgotten something. The next evening I was to host the County Hall dinner for the world of education in Leicestershire and Mr Lewis, who was a senior principal and about to retire, had been invited to make the speech in response to my few words of welcome to the guests.

So in my few after dinner words it seemed quite natural to inform such a gathering of my various visits to schools and in particular of the nostalgic day I had spent visiting the schools I had attended as a boy. I produced my City Boys registration card and said by way of a joke "thank goodness that is all the principal could find," only to notice the principal who was seated at my table reach down to take a file out of his briefcase. "That's what you think" he said, as he held up the brown manila file. I finished my few words and sat down and wondered what was to come.

It did not take too long to find out. He had found my school records in the vaults after I had left the previous day and proceeded to inform the assembled company of distinguished guests about them, the good and the bad. (No, there was nothing ugly!). The bad involved my detentions, far more than I ever remember! A detention was a punishment that involved staying behind after school for an hour. Apparently the records revealed that I even got a detention for talking in detention! However he was kind enough to find at least some good things and I took it all in good spirit. It certainly entertained our guests who found it hugely amusing.

The Department of Planning and Transportation was a very large department then, it has since downsized somewhat following the 1997 changes and we carried out a number of engagements to support the department during the year.

It would be difficult, even over a year, to bring to the attention of the public the many and diverse aspects of the service for which 'Tommy' Thompson, the Director, was responsible. I had

WITH HORACE SANKEY CC FOR THE DONISTHORPE RECLAMATION EVENT SPEECHES

a very early taste of the excellent 'nose' for publicity for which he was justifiably renowned when I was asked to drive a huge digger to mark the start of the reclamation works at the former Donisthorpe Colliery.

The naming ceremony of Sarahs Wood in the National Forest was another Department of Planning and Transportation event that was a huge PR success and the involvement of young Sarah Louise Goudie, after whom the wood was named, and the additional attraction of a TV personality Richard O'Brien, host of The Crystal Maze, brought the press and the television in droves.

'Tommy' Thompson was very anxious to publicise the work of his department in planning the transport needs of the County. To highlight the economic benefits of the rail link to the capital he arranged for me to ride in the cab of an Inter City 125 to London.

An exhilarating ride that offered an entirely different perspective into travelling by train which I enjoyed enormously. The driver was an 'old' rail man and talking about the way the railways are changing brought home to me just how much 'railwaymen' are attached to railways and how they regret all the change. The intention of the trip was that I ride in the cab to London and then eat lunch in the first class restaurant on the way back but I so enjoyed the experience and the conversation that I asked if I could return in the cab and this was agreed. My only real regret was that, for obvious reasons I was not allowed to drive the train, but I enjoyed the experience nevertheless.

Many other events were arranged to attract publicity to the road safety work that the County Council is actively involved in.

'Tommy' and his colleague officers were very proud of the Area Traffic Control to which I paid two visits during the civic year. The first was to have a good look at what had become one of the leading systems in the Country. Using a system of cameras and telephone lines a number of sensitive traffic spots could be 'dialed' up and viewed by the operator. They could also use the zoom facility at some locations and the images were clear enough to read number plates and faces of driver and passenger, quite amazing really that someone sitting in a control room in the middle of Leicester can see not only what cars have stopped at traffic lights in the middle of Melton Mowbray but can also know who is driving as well.

Unusually there two major road openings both of which for some reason caused some 'diplomatic' difficulties. Since the responsibility for road building had been handed to a new quango called the Highways Agency what used to be a simple organisational problem for the County Council had been turned into a major headache because everybody wanted to get in on the act. So, when the Northern Distributor Road, the A46, was opened the roads minister wanted to open it to demonstrate the governments commitment to road building, the local MP wanted to be involved to talk about getting a pedestrian bridge incorporated into the design and the local Mayor had to be involved and wanted to make a point about new roads saving lives and of course the Chairman of the County Council, me, must also say a few words. All this made for a very long ceremony, thank goodness the weather held and the day was a success.

Not so at the second opening. The Hinckley Northern Perimeter Road, which in any event was only about a mile long, was opened in driving rain and a howling wind and we all felt slightly ridiculous. The notes I had been given were soon so damp as to be useless, but even though there were no members of the public

A COLD AND RAINY DAY FOR THE OPENING OF THE HINCKLEY NORTHERN PERIMETER ROAD

present we all tumbled off the bus and did the opening properly. Though there was a slight diplomatic incident when in one of the speeches a dignitary thanked the wrong the contractor, for the excellent job they had done, and the contractor who had actually done the work, whose Managing Director was present, was not amused in the least.

As mentioned above my year as Chairman of the County Council ran in tandem with 'Tommy' Thompson being elected to the prestigious President of the County Surveyors Society, a great honour both for Tommy and the County Council. Naturally the Authority wanted to support Tommy fully in his year of office and it was agreed that the Chairman would host a Dinner and also speak at the Society Annual Dinner, which was to be held in London at the prestigious RAC Club.

The dinner in London was in the middle of January so we had only just returned from South Africa and sported a healthy tan, I think the after dinner words went well and I was followed by Sir George Young who was then Minister for Transport. The return dinner at County Hall was a great success and 'Tommy' was very pleased with the quality of the evening.

It was at one of Planning and Transportations events that I blotted my copybook and caused headlines by crossing Mr Gummer the then Minister of State for the Environment, the Minister primarily responsible for what in my opinion was the fiasco of Local Government Reform. The County Council had undertaken a significant project in an attempt to minimise waste and this had produced a good scheme that tackled the amount of paper and board and other material used by industry for wrapping and presenting their products, which the County Council as the waste disposal authority eventually had to dispose of.

Mr Gummer made a speech saying what a wonderful scheme this was, how important it was and praised the County Council for their excellent initiative and foresight.

Afterwards I just asked him why, if minimising waste was such a good idea, and the County Council was such a good one, was he about to abolish the County Council and waste six million pounds in the process. He blustered something about the County Council trying to deny Rutland its freedom so it deserved what was coming to it. All good stuff except that a journalist was listening and we made front page headlines in the local paper.

Not good!

I was after all on duty as Chairman and should not have allowed myself to get into such controversy. However Gummer, in my view, did not handle that re-organisation well, to say the least, and I simply could not help myself.

## Other Highlights

Every Chairman received an invitation to attend the annual re-enactment of the Battle of Bosworth at the battlefield site in Market Bosworth, but it occurred to me that more should be made of this occasion. I decided to invite some friends and neighbours and make a day of it and when I put the idea to the department they were very enthusiastic. I explained that I wanted to make it a family day and it was agreed that my guests would be a number of families with children, quite a lot actually, almost everyone from Martin Close, Stoney Stanton where we lived. We arranged for a buffet lunch with all the things that children like plus some attractions for children including face painting among others.

It turned out to be a wonderful afternoon and even some rain late on did not spoil the day. The last thing the chairman always does on this occasion is to take the salute when the battle is over but this time there was an unusual flavour to this moment. As I stood waiting for the parade to pass I was joined by two young ladies, each about seven years old, and when the officer lowered the lance by way of salute to 'The Chairman' he also lowered it to my two young friends the officer was gracious "my compliments to the ladies sire," he said. What a nice touch.

I was always very happy to visit libraries, literature and reading have been a passion of mine and I love libraries. So I really the celebrations of anniversaries at Great Glen, Knighton and Aylestone, which had been the library I had used as a child, a children's story telling session at the 'pork pie' library on Southfields Drive and other re-openings after refurbishment such as Evington.

There was also the mini words competition that, as Chairman, I was asked to judge alongside Chris Challis and the Literature Development Officer, Alison Dunne. There was also a very successful and innovative 'With Great Pleasure Event' at the Victoria

FAMILY AND FRIENDS AT THE BOSWORTH BATTLEFIELD EVENT

Room at the New Walk Museum, then the flagship of the integrated County Museum Service, when along with Jackie Strong, Chris Challis and others I read some of my favourite pieces of writing.

Each year the Fire Service invited the Chairman to visit the Central Fire Station on Lancaster Road, and I was also to visit Market Harborough and Hinckley Fire Stations. At Hinckley I was invited to try on the breathing apparatus the men wore when fire fighting and then to try a new system just developed. I was staggered at the difference, the equipment they were using, though efficient and reliable, was so very, very heavy whilst the new one was much lighter, and consequently safer to use. Apparently we had been unable to afford to replace the old equipment because of budget cuts. I wrote to all the party spokespersons on the Committee asking them to consider replacing the old breathing apparatus because of its ease of use and the enhanced safety it would give to fire-fighters. After some months this was done. If my intervention played any part in the decision to replace the old equipment I should have been pleased.

Norman Dickerson also arranged for me to try out the off road driving course at Bruntingthorpe. Very scary on a cold frosty

A VISIT TO THE BOOK BUS

morning driving up and down very steep and muddy hills and through water courses but I did it and was presented with a certificate by Norman Dickerson.

It was also the Fire Service Angling Club that was so helpful when I needed to organise the fishing competition to raise funds for the Sir Andrew Martin Trust for Young People, they also sent two teams and helped to make the business part of the competition go very well. Later, when I was no longer Chairman, I was flattered to be invited to the social evening when the Fire Service Angling Club presented prizes for that year's competitions. A very enjoyable evening full of banter and mickey taking, which included Norman Dickerson. He clearly enjoyed the confidence of his men and they obviously respected him enormously, a respect he reciprocated which his men appreciated. It was a highly professional and well managed service, thanks to Norman Dickerson.

We had one more, unscheduled, contact with the Fire Service, well just Blue Watch actually. One of the annual events hosted by every Chairman is a dinner at Castle House for County Dignitaries. So one evening in early May myself, Hilary with guests Lord Lieutenant and Lady, Bishop of Leicester and wife, Chief Constable and wife, High Sherriff and guest, actually Jean Lucas, who had stepped in at the last minute and so preserved the tradition of having fourteen at table in Castle House, were gathered for dinner, first course over waiting for the main when the fire alarm went off, apparently chef had created a lot of smoke in the kitchen which had triggered a sensitive alarm. This was relayed direct to Central Fire Station and as Castle House was a priority call out nothing could stop them, and they arrived bells clanging and then marched around the house for 10 or 15 minutes before accepting that it was an innocent false alarm. Still, it was quite embarrassing, though our guests enjoyed the diversion and no harm was done. Blue watch had demonstrated before the very eyes of 'County Dignitaries' how efficient they were and how quickly they could respond to a 'shout'.

Until I made an early morning visit to Melton Market I had no idea that there is always a Trading Standards Officer on duty on market day to make sure that the animals were 'fit for purpose' and that the descriptions given, say about the age of a horse, was genuine. I remember later that same day looking at the way Trading Standards Officers carry out their duties

around Melton. I followed two officers and saw the way they check the petrol pumps at garages to make sure that they were delivering a full gallon within the regulations. I also went to the offices at County Hall where scales could be checked.
The checking system was so sensitive that it could even measure the difference in weight between a blank piece of cardboard, and the same piece after I had signed it with a black crayon!

The Department confiscates a lot of counterfeit goods, much of which is put to good use. Some of the clothing was sent to orphanages in Romania and elsewhere and the audio tapes were handed over to the local Society for the Blind to be wiped and re used for recording talking newspapers for blind and partially sighted people.

# Chapter Four
# For Laura

When I became Chairman I had never heard of Laura Godby, maybe I should have because she only lived in the next village, and was already making a name for herself because she had raised a lot of sponsorship money for charity when she took part in the Bike-Aid event in Burbage.

The story starts when we were asked to open the Carnival at Sapcote, a village in my County Council patch and a village in which I had many friends. Then later on, and almost out of the blue, came an invitation to a wedding on the same day. It was from our oldest friends whose eldest son was to be married in north Derbyshire. So a dilemma, do we let the call of duty make us let down our oldest friends, and miss an important family celebration, as we had done with so many other personal things. We discussed it and agreed a compromise, I would honour the commitment to open the carnival and then travel up to the wedding to at least join our friends for the reception and Hilary would not attend the carnival so that she could go to the Church service for the wedding in the morning.

That meant of course that I would be unaccompanied for the whole of the Sapcote Carnival opening ceremony, and the thought occurred, this was a village carnival, why not a competition to find a Chairman's 'Lady for the Day', and when I telephoned the organisers to explain my dilemma and how we planned to ensure that between us Hilary and I would do both the wedding and the carnival, I also asked about a lady for the day. I should have known of course but they had already picked a Carnival Queen but they would think about the idea and let me know.

The Chairman rang back and said that she had spoken to Mrs Godby, Laura's mother who had agreed that Laura could become my Lady for the Day as long as I explained fully what was involved because, what she described as Laura's condition, meant that she could not walk far without help, and might need a wheelchair and that she soon got tired. I explained what I had in mind.

We had been told that as Chairman and Lady we would first judge the carnival floats then ride at the head of the carnival procession in a horse drawn carriage and when the procession reached the field we would open the carnival properly which would be supervised by Joe David a Tower of London Beefeater who was a well known town crier. I told Laura's mum that Laura could do just exactly what a Chairman's Lady would do, wear the chain of Office, be collected in the County Car and drive with the Chairman to where the carnival floats would gather, Judge the best float and then ride in the horse drawn carriage at the head of the procession with the chairman before jointly opening the carnival with the Chairman.

Laura had been chosen by the Carnival Committee even though she suffered with a rare and very serious progressive muscle wasting disease, the name of the disease is 'Pyruvite Hydrogenase deficiency was one I had never heard of. However disease or not Laura was already something of a local celebrity for a number of reasons. The Burbage Bike-Aid effort was her most recent achievement but the previous year she had gone to Florida with the group that provides holidays for children with life threatening medical conditions.

Laura's Mum agreed that she could accompany me at the Carnival and be my Lady for the Day and I sought her permission, which she gave, to issue a press release so that the carnival might get some free publicity.

The local press were very interested and a date for a photograph was arranged, which because I had not yet met Laura, would be our first meeting. I had little idea what to expect but in the event I needn't have worried, though Laura had plastic splints on her legs and because of her condition her speech is somewhat slurred I had some difficulty making out what she was saying, we got on very well right from the start. Her parents are really very down to earth and not over protective and very easy to get on with. Laura's a very pretty eleven year old and we set up in her garden for the photograph. What turned out was to be one of the best photographs of my civic year and was seen on the front page of both the local weekly newspaper and the leading daily in the County. It was also used on the inside cover of the Annual Report of the County Council. Laura certainly enjoyed being the centre of attraction and the publicity that followed from the photograph and the report of the lady for a day theme was appreciated by the carnival committee.

Come the day and everything worked out very well. The weather was perfect as we picked Laura up in the Daimler and we both judged the floats before joining the procession to the field where the main activities were to take place, not in a horse drawn carriage as first planned but in the County Car. Once on the field we opened the carnival and Laura was interviewed by local radio and Joe David in his wonderful booming voice declared the carnival open.

It was to prove to be one of the most successful carnivals on record for the amount of money collected and those organisations that benefited from a share of the money raised enjoyed something of a bonus that year. All of which made the whole day so very worthwhile and more than justified the lady for a day theme.

However that was not the end of my association with Laura for there is a sequel, and a nice one too!

Joe David, who had acted as Master of Ceremonies for the carnival, was at that time still a serving beefeater, or Yeoman Warder as it should be, at the Tower of London and he too had been captured by the personality and courage of this delightful young lady. It turned out that the Yeoman Warders have a charity to which they donate proceeds of various public appearances they all make from time to time and disburse to good causes as they are brought to their attention often in a very informal way. Joe had made enquiries about Laura and her mobility problem, which was getting worse as she lost the strength in her legs. More and more she had to use the wheelchair and Mum and Dad were the ones that had to push her about and she had little chance of independent travel. Joe had suggested to Laura's Mum and Dad that it might be possible for the Yeoman Warders charity to purchase an electrically driven wheelchair and give it to Laura if that would be acceptable to Laura and her parents.

Would it just!

They were hardly able to believe their luck and the Warders generosity.

So the Yeoman Warders invited Laura and her Mum and Dad down to the Tower of London, first to attend a service in the Chapel within the Tower, enjoy a VIP escorted trip around the Tower, have some lunch and then to be presented with the wheelchair.

On arrival at the Tower we were all given a VIP tour so we avoided all the queues and saw more than the average tourist would. We were taken to the Yeoman Warders social club which is of limits to the public and is full of the history of the Tower and has many interesting artefacts and covering the walls are original cartoons by all the famous newspaper cartoonists all of which featured either the Tower or the Beefeaters. The senior Yeoman Warder presented the wheelchair and it was interesting to note that there was no undue ceremony, no great fuss, just an incredibly generous act that would bring real benefit to Laura. The chair, which had cost almost £3000, was presented with an air of near embarrassment, as though the Beefeaters would have preferred just to send the chair and be done with it. We had a sandwich lunch before saying our goodbyes and set of for home.

Laura at my invitation also came to the Chairman's Christmas lunch for the staff near Christmas which I know she really enjoyed and afterwards I paid a visit to her school, Church Farm in Elmesthorpe where she is so very well looked after.

The way all her friends and the staff look after her at that school reflects great credit on them and I know it makes the problems that Laura's condition cause her to be that little bit more bearable.

# Chapter Five
# Postscript

The 26th March 1997 was to be the final meeting of the County Council created in 1973 by Act of Parliament and abolished in 1997 by Act of political spite. When the agenda for the meeting was published it was obvious that any chance of a dignified send off would not be possible, because by a trick of timing there was to be a general election in four weeks time so the debates would be laced with party political statements and rhetoric, with the elections for the new continuing County Council long planned for the same day. It was also the first meeting of the Council after the bitter and divisive County Council Budget meeting in February when thanks to the abstentions of Liberal Democrats the budget proposals of the Conservative group were adopted leaving the Labour group incandescent with rage and pledging to start the process of 'dismantling' what they perceived as the worst aspects of the budget at this the March meeting.

This meant that there would be no opportunity for members to pay tribute to colleagues and past and retiring officers for distinguished service and recording the achievements of the Council during its life because of this trick of timing. It was also the case that the Chairman, having agreed to make a civic visit to India, had chosen to pass on the duty of chairing this final council meeting to the Vice Chairman. Furthermore the Vice Chairman has been asked to represent the Chairman at the launch of the refitted HMS Quorn in Rosythe dockyard at 8am the following morning, and so was anxious to get away.

This anxiety, to be honest, showed during the meeting and became more apparent when the Labour group started what they promised was a series of motions, ten in all, which one by one would seek to restore funding to those voluntary groups which suffered in the previous months 'Tory' budget. Furthermore the Labour group made it clear that they would insist on a 'recorded vote' rather than the usual show of hands in order to make each of us put on public record how we had voted, a process which took much, much longer than the show of hands method.

The Vice Chairman, in the chair, seemed to let his anxiety to get away to Rosythe affect the conduct of the meeting and there were numerous bad tempered interventions which led to a fractious and ill tempered meeting. Suddenly, I was asked by the Liberal whip if, as the immediate past Chairman, I would be prepared to chair the rest of the meeting if the Vice Chairman felt he must leave to fulfil the engagement in Rosyth. I said I would, but only if the three group leaders agreed, as I would not submit to a vote. The Vice Chairman, in the chair, called a short adjournment and gained the agreement of the three leaders and I took the chair at about 7pm.

There was still much business to get through but we made progress and the mood lightened as motion followed motion, and as we reached the stage where the end was in sight I found myself thinking that as this was indeed the final meeting I should perhaps have some profound and meaningful final words to say. But I could not think of any and furthermore I thought it inappropriate for me who had branded the whole silly process of change as a farce to suddenly treat it seriously and say something deeply meaningful. So I did a deal with Anna Pullen, the member for Whetstone, who was quite a large lady, and wonderful with it, and who was quite prepared to own up to being 'fat'. I needed a 'fat' lady who would sing! Why! Because, mindful of the saying 'It's not over till the fat lady sings' all of us who had opposed the review now had to finally admit that it was indeed 'all over'.

So at the end of the final meeting of Leicestershire County Council 1973 to 1997 on the 26th March 1997 Councillor Anna Pullen, a fat lady by her own admission, stood up and sang Auld Lang Syne. Proof positive that it was indeed all over.

And it was all so unnecessary and to my mind a case study in bad government. How sad for me privately to have to admit that it was 'my' government that was the guilty party. And so the final irony, I who had opposed the changes with everything I could, in every way I could think of was sitting in the chair at the end of the final meeting.

*Life is indeed perplexing.*